# www.EffortlessMath.com

... So Much More Online!

✓ FREE Math lessons

✓ More Math learning books!

✓ Mathematics Worksheets

✓ Online Math Tutors

**Need a PDF version of this book?**

Please visit www.EffortlessMath.com

# ALEKS Math Prep 2020-2021

## The Most Comprehensive Review and Ultimate Guide to the ALEKS Math Test

By

Reza Nazari

All inquiries should be addressed to:

info@effortlessMath.com

www.EffortlessMath.com

**ISBN:** 978-1-64612-866-2

**Published by: Effortless Math Education**

**www.EffortlessMath.com**

**Visit www.EffortlessMath.com**

**for Online Math Practice**

## Description

***ALEKS Math Prep 2020 – 2021***, which reflects the 2020 - 2021 test guidelines, is dedicated to preparing test takers to ace the ALEKS Math Test. This comprehensive ALEKS Math Prep book with hundreds of examples, abundant sample ALEKS mathematics questions, and two full-length and realistic ALEKS Math tests is all you will ever need to fully prepare for the ALEKS Math. It will help you learn everything you need to ace the math section of the ALEKS test.

Effortless Math unique study program provides you with an in-depth focus on the math portion of the exam, helping you master the math skills that students find the most troublesome. This ALEKS Math preparation book contains most common sample questions that are most likely to appear in the mathematics section of the ALEKS.

Inside the pages of this comprehensive ALEKS Math book, students can learn basic math operations in a structured manner with a complete study program to help them understand essential math skills. It also has many exciting features, including:

- ✓ Content 100% aligned with the 2020 - 2021 ALEKS test
- ✓ Written by ALEKS Math instructors and test experts
- ✓ Complete coverage of all ALEKS Math concepts and topics which you will be tested
- ✓ Numerous ALEKS math practice questions in both multiple-choice and grid-in formats with answers grouped by topic, so you can focus on your weak areas
- ✓ Abundant Math skill building exercises to help test-takers approach different question types that might be *unfamiliar* to them
- ✓ Exercises on different ALEKS Math topics such as integers, percent, equations, polynomials, exponents and radicals
- ✓ 2 full-length practice tests (featuring new question types) with detailed answers

*ALEKS Mathematics Prep 2020 – 2021* is an incredibly useful resource for those who want to review all topics being covered on the ALEKS test. It efficiently and effectively reinforces learning outcomes through engaging questions and repeated practice, helping you to quickly master Math skills.

## About the Author

**Reza Nazari** is the author of more than 100 Math learning books including:
– **Math and Critical Thinking Challenges:** For the Middle and High School Student
– **ACT Math in 30 Days**
– **ASVAB Math Workbook 2018 - 2019**
– **Effortless Math Education Workbooks**
– **and many more Mathematics books ...**

Reza is also an experienced Math instructor and a test–prep expert who has been tutoring students since 2008. Reza is the founder of Effortless Math Education, a tutoring company that has helped many students raise their standardized test scores—and attend the colleges of their dreams. Reza provides an individualized custom learning plan and the personalized attention that makes a difference in how students view math.

You can contact Reza via email at:
reza@EffortlessMath.com

Find Reza's professional profile at:
goo.gl/zoC9rJ

# Content

# Chapter 1:

# Fractions and Mixed Numbers

---

**Math topics that you'll learn in this chapter:**

- ✓ Simplifying Fractions

- ✓ Adding and Subtracting Fractions

- ✓ Multiplying and Dividing Fractions

- ✓ Adding Mixed Numbers

- ✓ Subtracting Mixed Numbers

- ✓ Multiplying Mixed Numbers

- ✓ Dividing Mixed Numbers

# Simplifying Fractions

☑ A fraction contains two numbers separated by a bar between them. The bottom number, called the denominator, is the total number of equally divided portions in one whole. The top number, called the numerator, is how many portions you have. And the bar represents the operation of division.

☑ Simplifying a fraction means reducing it to the lowest terms. To simplify a fraction, evenly divide both the top and bottom of the fraction by $2, 3, 5, 7, \ldots$ etc.

☑ Continue until you can't go any further.

## Examples:

**1) Simplify** $\frac{12}{30}$

**Solution:** To simplify $\frac{12}{30}$, find a number that both 12 and 30 are divisible by.

Both are divisible by 6. Then: $\frac{12}{30} = \frac{12 \div 6}{30 \div 6} = \frac{2}{5}$

**2) Simplify** $\frac{64}{80}$

**Solution:** To simplify $\frac{64}{80}$, find a number that both 64 and 80 are divisible by.

Both are divisible by 8 and 16. Then: $\frac{64}{80} = \frac{64 \div 8}{80 \div 8} = \frac{8}{10}$, 8 and 10 are divisible by 2,

then: $\frac{8}{10} = \frac{4}{5}$ or $\frac{64}{80} = \frac{64 \div 16}{80 \div 16} = \frac{4}{5}$

**3) Simplify** $\frac{20}{60}$

**Solution:** To simplify $\frac{20}{60}$, find a number that both 20 and 60 are divisible by. Both are divisible by 20.

Then: $\frac{20}{60} = \frac{20 \div 20}{60 \div 20} = \frac{1}{3}$

# Adding and Subtracting Fractions

☑ For "like" fractions (fractions with the same denominator), add or subtract the numerators (top numbers) and write the answer over the common denominator (bottom numbers).

☑ Adding and Subtracting fractions with the same denominator:

$$\frac{a}{b} + \frac{c}{b} = \frac{a+c}{b} \qquad\qquad \frac{a}{b} - \frac{c}{b} = \frac{a-c}{b}$$

☑ Find equivalent fractions with the same denominator before you can add or subtract fractions with different denominators.

☑ Adding and Subtracting fractions with different denominators:

$$\frac{a}{b} + \frac{c}{d} = \frac{ad+bc}{bd} \qquad\qquad \frac{a}{b} - \frac{c}{d} = \frac{ad-bc}{bd}$$

## Examples:

1) Find the sum. $\dfrac{3}{4} + \dfrac{1}{3} =$

**Solution:** These two fractions are "unlike" fractions. (they have different denominators). Use this formula: $\dfrac{a}{b} + \dfrac{c}{d} = \dfrac{ad+cb}{bd}$

Then: $\dfrac{3}{4} + \dfrac{1}{3} = \dfrac{(3)(3)+(4)(1)}{4 \times 3} = \dfrac{9+4}{12} = \dfrac{13}{12}$

2) Find the difference. $\dfrac{4}{5} - \dfrac{3}{7} =$

**Solution:** For "unlike" fractions, find equivalent fractions with the same denominator before you can add or subtract fractions with different denominators. Use this formula:

$$\frac{a}{b} - \frac{c}{d} = \frac{ad-bc}{bd}$$

$$\frac{4}{5} - \frac{3}{7} = \frac{(4)(7)-(3)(5)}{5 \times 7} = \frac{28-15}{35} = \frac{13}{35}$$

ALEKS Mathematics Prep 2020-2021

# Multiplying and Dividing Fractions

☑ Multiplying fractions: multiply the top numbers and multiply the bottom numbers.

Simplify if necessary. $\frac{a}{b} \times \frac{c}{d} = \frac{a \times c}{b \times d}$

☑ Dividing fractions: Keep, Change, Flip

Keep the first fraction, change the division sign to multiplication, and flip the numerator and denominator of the second fraction. Then, solve!

$$\frac{a}{b} \div \frac{c}{d} = \frac{a}{b} \times \frac{d}{c} = \frac{a \times d}{b \times c}$$

## Examples:

1) Multiply. $\frac{5}{8} \times \frac{2}{3} =$

**Solution:** Multiply the top numbers and multiply the bottom numbers.

$\frac{5}{8} \times \frac{2}{3} = \frac{5 \times 2}{8 \times 3} = \frac{10}{24}$, simplify: $\frac{10}{24} = \frac{10 \div 2}{24 \div 2} = \frac{5}{12}$

2) Solve. $\frac{1}{3} \div \frac{4}{7} =$

**Solution:** Keep the first fraction, change the division sign to multiplication, and flip the numerator and denominator of the second fraction.

Then: $\frac{1}{3} \div \frac{4}{7} = \frac{1}{3} \times \frac{7}{4} = \frac{1 \times 7}{3 \times 4} = \frac{7}{12}$

3) Calculate. $\frac{3}{5} \times \frac{2}{3} =$

**Solution:** Multiply the top numbers and multiply the bottom numbers.

$\frac{3}{5} \times \frac{2}{3} = \frac{3 \times 2}{5 \times 3} = \frac{6}{15}$, simplify: $\frac{6}{15} = \frac{6 \div 3}{15 \div 3} = \frac{2}{5}$

4) Solve. $\frac{1}{4} \div \frac{5}{6} =$

**Solution:** Keep the first fraction, change the division sign to multiplication, and flip the numerator and denominator of the second fraction.

Then: $\frac{1}{4} \div \frac{5}{6} = \frac{1}{4} \times \frac{6}{5} = \frac{1 \times 6}{4 \times 5} = \frac{6}{20}$, simplify: $\frac{6}{20} = \frac{6 \div 2}{20 \div 2} = \frac{3}{10}$

# Adding Mixed Numbers

Use the following steps for adding mixed numbers:

☑ Add whole numbers of the mixed numbers.

☑ Add the fractions of the mixed numbers.

☑ Find the Least Common Denominator (LCD) if necessary.

☑ Add whole numbers and fractions.

☑ Write your answer in lowest terms.

## Examples:

1) Add mixed numbers.   $3\frac{1}{3} + 1\frac{4}{5} =$

   **Solution:** Let's rewriting our equation with parts separated, $3\frac{1}{3} + 1\frac{4}{5} = 3 + \frac{1}{3} + 1 + \frac{4}{5}$. Now, add whole number parts: $3 + 1 = 4$

   Add the fraction parts $\frac{1}{3} + \frac{4}{5}$. Rewrite to solve with the equivalent fractions. $\frac{1}{3} + \frac{4}{5} = \frac{5}{15} + \frac{12}{15} = \frac{17}{15}$. The answer is an improper fraction (numerator is bigger than denominator). Convert the improper fraction into a mixed number: $\frac{17}{15} = 1\frac{2}{15}$. Now, combine the whole and fraction parts: $4 + 1\frac{2}{15} = 5\frac{2}{15}$

2) Find the sum. $1\frac{2}{5} + 2\frac{1}{2} =$

   **Solution:** Rewriting our equation with parts separated, $1 + \frac{2}{5} + 2 + \frac{1}{2}$. Add the whole number parts:

   $1 + 2 = 3$. Add the fraction parts: $\frac{2}{5} + \frac{1}{2} = \frac{4}{10} + \frac{5}{10} = \frac{9}{10}$

   Now, combine the whole and fraction parts: $3 + \frac{9}{10} = 3\frac{9}{10}$

# Subtract Mixed Numbers

Use these steps for subtracting mixed numbers.

☑ Convert mixed numbers into improper fractions. $a\dfrac{c}{b} = \dfrac{ab+c}{b}$

☑ Find equivalent fractions with the same denominator for unlike fractions. (fractions with different denominators)

☑ Subtract the second fraction from the first one. $\dfrac{a}{b} - \dfrac{c}{d} = \dfrac{ad - bc}{bd}$

☑ Write your answer in lowest terms.

☑ If the answer is an improper fraction, convert it into a mixed number.

## Examples:

1) Subtract. $3\dfrac{4}{5} - 1\dfrac{3}{4} =$

**Solution:** Convert mixed numbers into fractions: $3\dfrac{4}{5} = \dfrac{3 \times 5 + 4}{5} = \dfrac{19}{5}$ and $1\dfrac{3}{4} = \dfrac{1 \times 4 + 3}{4} = \dfrac{7}{4}$
These two fractions are "unlike" fractions. (they have different denominators). Find equivalent fractions with the same denominator. Use this formula: $\dfrac{a}{b} - \dfrac{c}{d} = \dfrac{ad - bc}{bd}$
$\dfrac{19}{5} - \dfrac{7}{4} = \dfrac{(19)(4) - (5)(7)}{5 \times 4} = \dfrac{76 - 35}{20} = \dfrac{41}{20}$, the answer is an improper fraction, convert it into a mixed number. $\dfrac{41}{20} = 2\dfrac{1}{20}$

2) Subtract. $4\dfrac{3}{8} - 1\dfrac{1}{2} =$

**Solution:** Convert mixed numbers into fractions: $4\dfrac{3}{8} = \dfrac{4 \times 8 + 3}{8} = \dfrac{35}{8}$ and $1\dfrac{1}{2} = \dfrac{1 \times 2 + 1}{4} = \dfrac{3}{2}$
Find equivalent fractions: $\dfrac{3}{2} = \dfrac{12}{8}$. Then: $4\dfrac{3}{8} - 1\dfrac{1}{2} = \dfrac{35}{8} - \dfrac{12}{8} = \dfrac{23}{8}$
The answer is an improper fraction, convert it into a mixed number.
$$\dfrac{23}{8} = 2\dfrac{7}{8}$$

# Multiplying Mixed Numbers

Use the following steps for multiplying mixed numbers:

☑ Convert the mixed numbers into fractions. $a\frac{c}{b} = a + \frac{c}{b} = \frac{ab+c}{b}$

☑ Multiply fractions. $\frac{a}{b} \times \frac{c}{d} = \frac{a \times c}{b \times d}$

☑ Write your answer in lowest terms.

☑ If the answer is an improper fraction (numerator is bigger than denominator), convert it into a mixed number.

## Examples:

1) Multiply. $3\frac{1}{3} \times 4\frac{1}{6} =$

   **Solution:** Convert mixed numbers into fractions, $3\frac{1}{3} = \frac{3 \times 3 + 1}{3} = \frac{10}{3}$ and $4\frac{1}{6} = \frac{4 \times 6 + 1}{6} = \frac{25}{6}$

   Apply the fractions rule for multiplication, $\frac{10}{3} \times \frac{25}{6} = \frac{10 \times 25}{3 \times 6} = \frac{250}{18}$

   The answer is an improper fraction. Convert it into a mixed number. $\frac{250}{18} = 13\frac{8}{9}$

2) Multiply. $2\frac{1}{2} \times 3\frac{2}{3} =$

   **Solution:** Converting mixed numbers into fractions, $2\frac{1}{2} \times 3\frac{2}{3} = \frac{5}{2} \times \frac{11}{3}$

   Apply the fractions rule for multiplication, $\frac{5}{2} \times \frac{11}{3} = \frac{5 \times 11}{2 \times 3} = \frac{55}{6} = 9\frac{1}{6}$

3) Multiply mixed numbers. $2\frac{1}{3} \times 2\frac{1}{2} =$

   **Solution:** Converting mixed numbers to fractions, $2\frac{1}{3} = \frac{7}{3}$ and $2\frac{1}{2} = \frac{5}{2}$. Multiply two fractions:

   $$\frac{7}{3} \times \frac{5}{2} = \frac{7 \times 5}{3 \times 2} = \frac{35}{6} = 5\frac{5}{6}$$

# Dividing Mixed Numbers

Use the following steps for dividing mixed numbers:

☑ Convert the mixed numbers into fractions. $a\frac{c}{b} = a + \frac{c}{b} = \frac{ab+c}{b}$

☑ Divide fractions: Keep, Change, Flip: Keep the first fraction, change the division sign to multiplication, and flip the numerator and denominator of the second fraction. Then, solve!   $\frac{a}{b} \div \frac{c}{d} = \frac{a}{b} \times \frac{d}{c} = \frac{a \times d}{b \times c}$

☑ Write your answer in lowest terms.

☑ If the answer is an improper fraction (numerator is bigger than denominator), convert it into a mixed number.

## Examples:

1) Solve. $3\frac{2}{3} \div 2\frac{1}{2}$

**Solution:** Convert mixed numbers into fractions: $3\frac{2}{3} = \frac{3 \times 3 + 2}{3} = \frac{11}{3}$ and $2\frac{1}{2} = \frac{2 \times 2 + 1}{2} = \frac{5}{2}$

Keep, Change, Flip: $\frac{11}{3} \div \frac{5}{2} = \frac{11}{3} \times \frac{2}{5} = \frac{11 \times 2}{3 \times 5} = \frac{22}{15}$. The answer is an improper fraction. Convert it into a mixed number: $\frac{22}{15} = 1\frac{7}{15}$

2) Solve. $3\frac{4}{5} \div 1\frac{5}{6}$

**Solution:** Convert mixed numbers to fractions, then solve:

$3\frac{4}{5} \div 1\frac{5}{6} = \frac{19}{5} \div \frac{11}{6} = \frac{19}{5} \times \frac{6}{11} = \frac{114}{55} = 2\frac{4}{55}$

3) Solve. $2\frac{2}{7} \div 2\frac{3}{5}$

**Solution:** Converting mixed numbers to fractions: $3\frac{4}{5} \div 1\frac{5}{6} = \frac{16}{7} \div \frac{13}{5}$

Keep, Change, Flip: $\frac{16}{7} \div \frac{13}{5} = \frac{16}{7} \times \frac{5}{13} = \frac{16 \times 5}{7 \times 13} = \frac{80}{91}$

# Chapter 1: Practices

✎ *Simplify each fraction.*

1) $\frac{18}{30} =$

2) $\frac{21}{42} =$

3) $\frac{35}{55} =$

4) $\frac{48}{72} =$

5) $\frac{54}{81} =$

6) $\frac{80}{200} =$

✎ *Find the sum or difference.*

7) $\frac{6}{15} + \frac{3}{15} =$ $\frac{6}{15}$

8) $\frac{2}{3} + \frac{1}{9} =$

9) $\frac{1}{4} + \frac{2}{5} =$

10) $\frac{7}{10} - \frac{3}{10} =$

11) $\frac{1}{2} - \frac{3}{8} =$

12) $\frac{5}{7} - \frac{3}{5} =$

✎ *Find the answers.*

13) $\frac{1}{7} \div \frac{3}{8} =$

14) $\frac{2}{3} \times \frac{4}{7} =$

15) $\frac{5}{7} \times \frac{3}{4} =$

16) $\frac{2}{5} \div \frac{3}{7} =$

17) $\frac{3}{7} \div \frac{5}{8} =$ $\frac{15}{56}$

18) $\frac{3}{8} \times \frac{4}{7} =$

✎ *Calculate.*

19) $3\frac{1}{5} + 2\frac{2}{9} =$

20) $1\frac{1}{7} + 5\frac{2}{5} =$

21) $4\frac{4}{5} + 1\frac{2}{7} =$

22) $2\frac{4}{7} + 2\frac{3}{5} =$

23) $1\frac{5}{6} + 1\frac{2}{5} =$

24) $3\frac{5}{7} + 1\frac{2}{9} =$

## ✎ Calculate.

25) $3\frac{2}{5} - 1\frac{2}{9} =$

27) $4\frac{2}{5} - 2\frac{2}{7} =$

29) $9\frac{5}{7} - 7\frac{4}{21} =$

26) $5\frac{3}{5} - 1\frac{1}{7} =$

28) $8\frac{3}{4} - 2\frac{1}{8} =$

30) $11\frac{7}{12} - 9\frac{5}{6} =$

## ✎ Find the answers.

31) $1\frac{1}{8} \times 1\frac{3}{4} =$

33) $2\frac{1}{8} \times 1\frac{2}{9} = \dfrac{187}{72}$

35) $1\frac{1}{2} \times 5\frac{2}{3} =$

32) $3\frac{1}{5} \times 2\frac{2}{7} =$

34) $2\frac{3}{8} \times 2\frac{2}{5} =$

36) $3\frac{1}{2} \times 6\frac{2}{3} =$

## ✎ Solve.

37) $9\frac{1}{2} \div 2\frac{3}{5} =$

39) $5\frac{3}{4} \div 2\frac{2}{7} =$

41) $7\frac{2}{5} \div 3\frac{3}{4} =$

38) $2\frac{3}{8} \div 1\frac{2}{5} =$

40) $8\frac{1}{3} \div 4\frac{1}{4} =$

42) $2\frac{4}{5} \div 3\frac{2}{3} =$

# Answers – Chapter 1

1) $\frac{3}{5}$

2) $\frac{1}{2}$

3) $\frac{7}{11}$

4) $\frac{2}{3}$

5) $\frac{2}{3}$

6) $\frac{2}{5}$

7) $\frac{3}{5}$

8) $\frac{7}{9}$

9) $\frac{13}{20}$

10) $\frac{2}{5}$

11) $\frac{1}{8}$

12) $\frac{4}{35}$

13) $\frac{8}{21}$

14) $\frac{8}{21}$

15) $\frac{15}{28}$

16) $\frac{14}{15}$

17) $\frac{24}{35}$

18) $\frac{3}{14}$

19) $5\frac{19}{45}$

20) $6\frac{19}{35}$

21) $6\frac{3}{35}$

22) $5\frac{6}{35}$

23) $3\frac{7}{30}$

24) $4\frac{59}{63}$

25) $2\frac{8}{45}$

26) $6\frac{16}{35}$

27) $2\frac{4}{35}$

28) $6\frac{5}{8}$

29) $2\frac{11}{21}$

30) $1\frac{3}{4}$

31) $1\frac{31}{32}$

32) $7\frac{11}{35}$

33) $2\frac{43}{72}$

34) $5\frac{7}{10}$

35) $8\frac{1}{2}$

36) $23\frac{1}{3}$

37) $3\frac{17}{26}$

38) $1\frac{39}{56}$

39) $2\frac{33}{64}$

40) $1\frac{49}{51}$

41) $1\frac{73}{75}$

42) $\frac{42}{55}$

# Chapter 2:

# Decimals

---

**Math topics that you'll learn in this chapter:**

- ✓ Comparing Decimals

- ✓ Rounding Decimals

- ✓ Adding and Subtracting Decimals

- ✓ Multiplying and Dividing Decimals

# Comparing Decimals

- A decimal is a fraction written in a special form. For example, instead of writing $\frac{1}{2}$ you can write $0.5$

- A Decimal Number contains a Decimal Point. It separates the whole number part from the fractional part of a decimal number.

- Let's review decimal place values: Example: $53.9861$

  5: tens        3: ones        9: tenths

  8: hundredths        6: thousandths        1: tens thousandths

☑ To compare decimals, compare each digit of two decimals in the same place value. Start from left. Compare hundreds, tens, ones, tenth, hundredth, etc.

☑ To compare numbers, use these symbols:

Equal to $=$        Less than $<$      Greater than $>$
Greater than or equal $\geq$      Less than or equal $\leq$

## Examples:

1) Compare $0.60$ and $0.06$.

   **Solution:** $0.60$ *is greater than* $0.06$, because the tenth place of $0.60$ is 6, but the tenth place of $0.06$ is zero. Then: $0.60 > 0.06$

2) Compare $0.0815$ and $0.815$.

   **Solution:** $0.815$ *is greater than* $0.0815$, because the tenth place of $0.815$ is 8, but the tenth place of $0.0815$ is zero. Then: $0.0815 < 0.815$

# Rounding Decimals

☑ We can round decimals to a certain accuracy or number of decimal places. This is used to make calculations easier to do and results easier to understand, when exact values are not too important.

☑ First, you'll need to remember your place values: For example:

$$12.4869$$

| 1: tens | 2: ones | 4: tenths |
| 8: hundredths | 6: thousandths | 9: tens thousandths |

☑ To round a decimal, first find the place value you'll round to.

☑ Find the digit to the right of the place value you're rounding to. If it is 5 or bigger, add 1 to the place value you're rounding to and remove all digits on its right side. If the digit to the right of the place value is less than 5, keep the place value and remove all digits on the right.

## Examples:

1) Round $1.9278$ to the thousandth place value.

**Solution:** First look at the next place value to the right, (tens thousandths). It's 8 and it is greater than 5. Thus add 1 to the digit in the thousandth place. The thousandth place is 7. $\rightarrow 7 + 1 = 8$, then, the answer is 1.928

2) Round $9.4126$ to the nearest hundredth.

**Solution:** First, look at the digit to the right of hundredth (thousandths place value). It's 2 and it is less than 5, thus remove all the digits to the right of hundredth place. Then, the answer is 9.41

# Adding and Subtracting Decimals

✅ Line up the decimal numbers.

✅ Add zeros to have the same number of digits for both numbers if necessary.

✅ Remember your place values: For example:

$$73.5196$$

7: tens      3: ones      5: tenths

1: hundredths      9: thousandths      6: tens thousandths

✅ Add or subtract using column addition or subtraction.

## Examples:

1) Add. $1.8 + 3.12$

**Solution:** First, line up the numbers: $\begin{array}{r} 1.8 \\ +\ 3.12 \\ \hline \end{array}$ → Add a zero to have the same number of digits for both numbers. $\begin{array}{r} 1.80 \\ +\ 3.12 \\ \hline \end{array}$ → Start with the hundredths place: $0 + 2 = 2$, $\begin{array}{r} 1.80 \\ +\ 3.12 \\ \hline 2 \end{array}$ → Continue with tenths place: $8 + 1 = 9$, $\begin{array}{r} 1.80 \\ +\ 3.12 \\ \hline .92 \end{array}$ → Add the ones place: $3 + 1 = 4$, $\begin{array}{r} 1.80 \\ +\ 3.12 \\ \hline 4.92 \end{array}$

2) Find the difference. $3.67 - 2.23$

**Solution:** First, line up the numbers: $\begin{array}{r} 3.67 \\ -\ 2.23 \\ \hline \end{array}$ → Start with the hundredths place: $7 - 3 = 4$, $\begin{array}{r} 3.67 \\ -\ 2.23 \\ \hline 4 \end{array}$ → Continue with tenths place. $6 - 2 = 4$, $\begin{array}{r} 3.67 \\ -\ 2.23 \\ \hline .44 \end{array}$ → Subtract the ones place. $3 - 2 = 1$, $\begin{array}{r} 3.67 \\ -\ 2.23 \\ \hline 1.44 \end{array}$

# Multiplying and Dividing Decimals

**For multiplying decimals:**

☑ Ignore the decimal point and set up and multiply the numbers as you do with whole numbers.

☑ Count the total number of decimal places in both of the factors.

☑ Place the decimal point in the product.

**For dividing decimals:**

☑ If the divisor is not a whole number, move the decimal point to the right to make it a whole number. Do the same for the dividend.

☑ Divide similar to whole numbers.

## Examples:

1) Find the product. $0.81 \times 0.32 =$

   **Solution:** Set up and multiply the numbers as you do with whole numbers. Line up the numbers: $\begin{array}{r} 81 \\ \times 32 \end{array}$ → Start with the ones place then continue with other digits → $\frac{\begin{array}{r} 81 \\ \times 32 \end{array}}{2,592}$. Count the total number of decimal places in both of the factors. There are four decimals digits. (two for each factor 0.81 and 0.32) Then: $0.81 \times 0.32 = 0.2592$

2) Find the quotient. $1.60 \div 0.4 =$

   **Solution:** The divisor is not a whole number. Multiply it by 10 to get 4: → $0.4 \times 10 = 4$

   Do the same for the dividend to get 16. → $1.60 \times 10 = 1.6$

   Now, divide: $16 \div 4 = 4$. The answer is 4.

# Chapter 2: Practices

✎ *Compare. Use >, =, and <*

1) 0.88 $\boxed{>}$ 0.088    3) 0.99 $\square$ 0.89    5) 1.58 $\boxed{<}$ 1.75

2) 0.56 $\square$ 0.57    4) 1.55 $\square$ 1.65    6) 2.91 $\boxed{>}$ 2.85

✎ *Round each decimal to the nearest whole number.*

7) 5.94    9) 9.7    11) 24.46  24

8) 16.47    10) 35.8    12) 12.5  13

✎ *Find the sum or difference.*

64.48

13)  $43.15 + 23.65 =$    15)  $25.47 + 31.76 =$    17)  $45.53 + 18.95 =$

14)  $56.74 - 22.43 =$    16)  $69.87 - 35.98 =$    18)  $25.13 - 18.72 =$

✎ *Find the product and quotient.*

19) $0.5 \times 0.8 =$    21) $3.25 \times 2.2 =$    23) $5.4 \times 0.6 =$

20) $6.4 \div 0.4 =$    22) $8.4 \div 2.5 =$    24) $1.42 \div 0.5 =$

# Answers – Chapter 2

1) $0.88 > 0.088$

2) $0.56 < 0.57$

3) $0.99 > 0.89$

4) $1.55 < 1.65$

5) $1.58 < 1.75$

6) $2.91 > 2.85$

7) 6

8) 16

9) 10

10) 36

11) 24

12) 13

13) 66.8

14) 34.31

15) 57.23

16) 33.89

17) 64.48

18) 6.41

19) 0.4

20) 16

21) 7.15

22) 3.36

23) 3.24

24) 2.84

# Chapter 3:

# Integers and Order of Operations

**Math topics that you'll learn in this chapter:**

- ✓ Adding and Subtracting Integers

- ✓ Multiplying and Dividing Integers

- ✓ Order of Operations

- ✓ Integers and Absolute Value

# Adding and Subtracting Integers

☑ Integers include zero, counting numbers, and the negative of the counting numbers. $\{... , -3, -2, -1, 0, 1, 2, 3, ...\}$

☑ Add a positive integer by moving to the right on the number line. (you will get a bigger number)

☑ Add a negative integer by moving to the left on the number line. (you will get a smaller number)

☑ Subtract an integer by adding its opposite.

## Examples:

1) Solve. $(-4) - (-5) =$

   **Solution:** Keep the first number and convert the sign of the second number to its opposite. (change subtraction into addition. Then: $(-4) + 5 = 1$

2) Solve. $11 + (8 - 19) =$

   **Solution:** First, subtract the numbers in brackets, $8 - 19 = -11$.

   Then: $11 + (-11) = \rightarrow$ change addition into subtraction: $11 - 11 = 0$

3) Solve. $5 - (-14 - 3) =$

   **Solution:** First, subtract the numbers in brackets, $-14 - 3 = -17$

   Then: $5 - (-17) = \rightarrow$ change subtraction into addition: $5 + 17 = 22$

4) Solve. $10 + (-6 - 15) =$

   **Solution:** First, subtract the numbers in brackets, $-6 - 15 = -21$

   Then: $10 + (-21) = \rightarrow$ change addition into subtraction: $10 - 21 = -11$

# Multiplying and Dividing Integers

Use the following rules for multiplying and dividing integers:

- ☑ (negative) × (negative) = positive

- ☑ (negative) ÷ (negative) = positive

- ☑ (negative) × (positive) = negative

- ☑ (negative) ÷ (positive) = negative

- ☑ (positive) × (positive) = positive

- ☑ (positive) ÷ (negative) = negative

## Examples:

1) Solve. $2 \times (-3) =$

**Solution:** Use this rule: (positive) × (negative) = negative.
Then: $(2) \times (-3) = -6$

2) Solve. $(-5) + (-27 \div 9) =$

**Solution:** First, divide $-27$ by 9, the numbers in brackets, use this rule:
(negative) ÷ (positive) = negative. Then: $-27 \div 9 = -3$
$(-5) + (-27 \div 9) = (-5) + (-3) = -5 - 3 = -8$

3) Solve. $(15 - 17) \times (-8) =$

**Solution:** First, subtract the numbers in brackets, $15 - 17 = -2 \rightarrow (-2) \times (-8) =$

Now use this rule: (negative) × (negative) = positive
$(-2) \times (-8) = 16$

4) Solve. $(16 - 10) \div (-2) =$

**Solution:** First, subtract the numbers in brackets, $16 - 10 = 6 \rightarrow (6) \div (-2) =$

Now use this rule: (positive) ÷ (negative) = negative
$(6) \div (-2) = -3$

# Order of Operations

☑ In Mathematics, "operations" are addition, subtraction, multiplication, division, exponentiation (written as $b^n$), and grouping;

☑ When there is more than one math operation in an expression, use PEMDAS: (to memorize this rule, remember the phrase "Please Excuse My Dear Aunt Sally".)

   ❖ Parentheses
   ❖ Exponents
   ❖ Multiplication and Division (from left to right)
   ❖ Addition and Subtraction (from left to right)

## Examples:

1) Calculate. $(3 + 5) \div (3^2 \div 9) =$

   **Solution:** First, simplify inside parentheses: $(8) \div (9 \div 9) = (8) \div (1)$, Then: $(8) \div (1) = 8$

2) Solve. $(7 \times 8) - (12 - 4) =$

   **Solution:** First, calculate within parentheses: $(7 \times 8) - (12 - 4) = (56) - (8)$, Then: $(56) - (8) = 48$

3) Calculate. $-2[(8 \times 9) \div (2^2 \times 2)] =$

   **Solution:** First, calculate within parentheses: $-2[(72) \div (4 \times 2)] = -2[(72) \div (8)] = -2[9]$ multiply $-2$ and 9. Then: $-2[9] = -18$

4) Solve. $(14 \div 7) + (-13 + 8) =$

   **Solution:** First, calculate within parentheses: $(14 \div 7) + (-13 + 8) = (2) + (-5)$

   Then: $(2) - (5) = -3$

# Integers and Absolute Value

- ☑ The absolute value of a number is its distance from zero, in either direction, on the number line. For example, the distance of 9 and −9 from zero on number line is 9.

- ☑ The absolute value of an integer is the numerical value without its sign. (negative or positive)

- ☑ The vertical bar is used for absolute value as in $|x|$.

- ☑ The absolute value of a number is never negative; because it only shows, "how far the number is from zero".

## Examples:

1) Calculate. $|12 - 4| \times 4 =$

   **Solution:** First, solve $|12 - 4|$, → $|12 - 4| = |8|$, the absolute value of 8 is 8, $|8| = 8$
   Then: $8 \times 4 = 32$

2) Solve. $\frac{|-16|}{4} \times |3 - 8| =$

   **Solution:** First, find $|-16|$, → the absolute value of −16 is 16, then: $|-16| = 16$,
   $\frac{16}{4} \times |3 - 8| =$
   Now, calculate $|3 - 8|$, → $|3 - 8| = |-5|$, the absolute value of −5 is 5. $|-5| = 5$
   Then: $\frac{16}{4} \times 5 = 4 \times 5 = 20$

3) Solve. $|9 - 3| \times \frac{|-3 \times 8|}{6} =$

   **Solution:** First, calculate $|9 - 3|$, → $|9 - 3| = |6|$, the absolute value of 6 is 6, $|6| = 6$. Then:
   $6 \times \frac{|-3 \times 8|}{6}$
   Now calculate $|-3 \times 8|$, → $|-3 \times 8| = |-24|$, the absolute value of −24 is 24, $|-24| = 24$
   Then: $6 \times \frac{24}{6} = 6 \times 4 = 24$

# Chapter 3: Practices

✍ *Find each sum or difference.*

1) $18 + (-5) =$ $13$

2) $(-16) + 24 =$

3) $(-12) + (-9) =$

4) $14 + (-8) + 6 =$

5) $24 + (-10 - 7) =$

6) $(-15) + (-6 + 12) =$

✍ *Find each product or quotient.*

7) $8 \times (-6) =$

8) $(-12) \div (-3) =$

9) $(-4) \times (-7) \times 2 =$

10) $3 \times (-5) \times (-6) =$

11) $(-7 - 37) \div (-11) =$

12) $(8 - 6) \times (-24) =$

✍ *Evaluate each expression.*

13) $8 + (3 \times 7) =$

14) $(18 \times 2) - 14 =$

15) $(15 - 7) + (2 \times 6) =$

16) $(8 + 4) \div (2^3 \div 2) =$

17) $2[(6 \times 3) \div (3^2 \times 2)] =$ $2$

18) $-3[(8 \times 2^2) \div (8 \times 2)] =$

✍ *Find the answers.*

19) $|-6| + |9 - 12| =$

20) $|8| - |7 - 19| + 1 =$ $-3$

21) $\frac{|-4|}{8} \times \frac{|-15|}{5} =$

22) $|7 \times -5| \times \frac{|-32|}{8} =$

23) $\frac{|-121|}{11} - |-8 \times 2| =$

24) $\frac{|-3 \times -6|}{9} \times \frac{|4 \times -6|}{8} =$ $6$

# Answers – Chapter 3

1) 13
2) 8
3) −21
4) 12
5) 7
6) −9
7) −48
8) 4
9) 56
10) 90
11) 4
12) −48

13) 29
14) 22
15) 20
16) 3
17) 2
18) −6
19) 9
20) −3
21) 15
22) 140
23) −5
24) 6

# Chapter 4:

# Ratios and Proportions

**Math topics that you'll learn in this chapter:**

- ✓ Simplifying Ratios

- ✓ Proportional Ratios

- ✓ Similarity and Ratios

# Simplifying Ratios

✓ Ratios are used to make comparisons between two numbers.

✓ Ratios can be written as a fraction, using the word "to", or with a colon.
Example: $\frac{3}{4}$ or "3 to 4" or $3:4$

✓ You can calculate equivalent ratios by multiplying or dividing both sides of the ratio by the same number.

## Examples:

1) Simplify. $9:3 =$

   **Solution:** Both numbers 9 and 3 are divisible by 3 , $\Rightarrow 9 \div 3 = 3,$ $\qquad 3 \div 3 = 1$, Then: $9:3 = 3:1$

2) Simplify. $\frac{24}{44} =$

   **Solution:** Both numbers 24 and 44 are divisible by 4, $\Rightarrow 24 \div 4 = 6, 44 \div 4 = 11$, Then: $\frac{24}{44} = \frac{6}{11}$

3) There are 36 students in a class and 16 are girls. Write the ratio of girls to boys.

   **Solution:** Subtract 16 from 36 to find the number of boys in the class. $36 - 16 = 20$. There are 20 boys in the class. So, the ratio of girls to boys is $16:20$. Now, simplify this ratio. Both 20 and 16 are divisible by 4. Then: $20 \div 4 = 5$, and $16 \div 4 = 4$. In the simplest form, this ratio is $4:5$

4) A recipe calls for butter and sugar in the ratio $3:4$. If you're using 9 cups of butter, how many cups of sugar should you use?

   **Solution:** Since, you use 9 cups of butter, or 3 times as much, you need to multiply the amount of sugar by 3. Then: $4 \times 3 = 12$. So, you need to use 12 cups of sugar. You can solve this using equivalent fractions: $\frac{3}{4} = \frac{9}{12}$

# Proportional Ratios

☑ Two ratios are proportional if they represent the same relationship.

☑ A proportion means that two ratios are equal. It can be written in two

  ways:   $\frac{a}{b} = \frac{c}{d}$      $a : b = c : d$

☑ The proportion $\frac{a}{b} = \frac{c}{d}$ can be written as: $a \times d = c \times b$

## Examples:

1) Solve this proportion for $x$. $\frac{3}{7} = \frac{12}{x}$

   **Solution:** Use cross multiplication: $\frac{3}{7} = \frac{12}{x} \Rightarrow 3 \times x = 7 \times 12 \Rightarrow 3x = 84$

   Divide both sides by 3 to find $x$:   $x = \frac{84}{3} \Rightarrow x = 28$

2) If a box contains red and blue balls in ratio of $3 : 7$ red to blue, how many red
   balls are there if $49$ blue balls are in the box?

   **Solution:** Write a proportion and solve. $\frac{3}{7} = \frac{x}{49}$

   Use cross multiplication: $3 \times 49 = 7 \times x \Rightarrow 147 = 7x$

   Divide to find $x$:   $x = \frac{147}{7} \Rightarrow x = 21$. There are 21 red balls in the box.

3) Solve this proportion for $x$. $\frac{2}{9} = \frac{12}{x}$

   **Solution:** Use cross multiplication:   $\frac{2}{9} = \frac{12}{x} \Rightarrow 2 \times x = 9 \times 12 \Rightarrow 2x = 108$

   Divide to find $x$:   $x = \frac{108}{2} \Rightarrow x = 54$

4) Solve this proportion for $x$. $\frac{6}{7} = \frac{18}{x}$

   **Solution:** Use cross multiplication:   $\frac{6}{7} = \frac{18}{x} \Rightarrow 6 \times x = 7 \times 18 \Rightarrow 6x = 126$

   Divide to find $x$:   $x = \frac{126}{6} \Rightarrow x = 21$

# Similarity and Ratios

☑ Two figures are similar if they have the same shape.

☑ Two or more figures are similar if the corresponding angles are equal, and the corresponding sides are in proportion.

## Examples:

1) The following triangles are similar. What is the value of the unknown side?

**Solution:** Find the corresponding sides and write a proportion.

$\frac{5}{10} = \frac{4}{x}$. Now, use the cross product to solve for $x$:

$\frac{5}{10} = \frac{4}{x} \rightarrow 5 \times x = 10 \times 4 \rightarrow 5x = 40$. Divide

both sides by 5. Then: $5x = 40 \rightarrow \frac{5x}{5} = \frac{40}{5} \rightarrow x = 8$

The missing side is 8.

 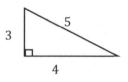

2) Two rectangles are similar. The first is 6 feet wide and 20 feet long. The second is 15 feet wide. What is the length of the second rectangle?

**Solution:** Let's put $x$ for the length of the second rectangle. Since two rectangles are similar, their corresponding sides are in proportion. Write a proportion and solve for the missing number. $\frac{6}{15} = \frac{20}{x} \rightarrow 6x = 15 \times 20 \rightarrow 6x = 300 \rightarrow x = \frac{300}{6} = 50$

The length of the second rectangle is 50 feet.

# Chapter 4: Practices

✎ *Reduce each ratio.*

1) $9:18 = \underline{1}:\underline{2}$

2) $6:54 = \underline{1}:\underline{4}$

3) $28:49 = \underline{\quad}:\underline{\quad}$

4) Bob has 12 red cards and 20 green cards. What is the ratio of Bob's red cards to his green cards? _____

5) In a party, 10 soft drinks are required for every 12 guests. If there are 252 guests, how many soft drinks is required? _____

6) In Jack's class, 18 of the students are tall and 10 are short. In Michael's class 54 students are tall and 30 students are short. Which class has a higher ratio of tall to short students? _____

✎ *Solve each proportion.*

7) $\frac{3}{7} = \frac{18}{x}, x = \underline{\quad}$

8) $\frac{5}{9} = \frac{x}{108}, x = \underline{\quad}$

9) $\frac{2}{13} = \frac{8}{x}, x = \underline{52}$

10) $\frac{4}{10} = \frac{6}{x}, x = \underline{15}$

11) $\frac{8}{20} = \frac{x}{65}, x = \underline{\quad}$

12) $\frac{6}{15} = \frac{14}{x}, x = \underline{\quad}$

✎ *Solve each problem.*

13) Two rectangles are similar. The first is $8\,feet$ wide and $22\,feet$ long. The second is $12\,feet$ wide. What is the length of the second rectangle? _____ 33 feet

14) Two rectangles are similar. One is $3.2\,meters$ by $8\,meters$. The longer side of the second rectangle is $34.5\,meters$. What is the other side of the second rectangle? _____

# Answers – Chapter 4

1) 1:2

2) 1:9

3) 4:7

4) 3:5

5) 210

6) The ratio for both classes is 9 to 5.

7) 42

8) 60

9) 52

10) 15

11) 26

12) 35

13) 33 feet

14) 13.8 meters

# Chapter 5:

# Percentage

---

**Math topics that you'll learn in this chapter:**

✓ Percentage Calculations

✓ Percent Problems

✓ Percent of Increase and Decrease

✓ Discount, Tax and Tip

✓ Simple Interest

# Percent Problems

☑ Percent is a ratio of a number and 100. It always has the same denominator, 100. The percent symbol is "%".

☑ Percent means "per 100". So, 20% is 20/100.

☑ In each percent problem, we are looking for the base, or part or the percent.

☑ Use these equations to find each missing section in a percent problem:

- o Base = Part ÷ Percent
- o Part = Percent × Base
- o Percent = Part ÷ Base

## Examples:

1) What is 25% of 60?

**Solution:** In this problem, we have percent (25%) and base (60) and we are looking for the "part".

Use this formula: $part = percent \times base$. Then: $part = 25\% \times 60 = \frac{25}{100} \times 60 = 0.25 \times 60 = 15$.

The answer:

25% of 60 is 15.

2) 20 is what percent of 400?

**Solution:** In this problem, we are looking for the percent. Use this equation:

$Percent = Part \div Base \rightarrow Percent = 20 \div 400 = 0.05 = 5\%$.

Then: 20 is 5 percent of 400.

# Percent of Increase and Decrease

☑ Percent of change (increase or decrease) is a mathematical concept that represents the degree of change over time.

☑ To find the percentage of increase or decrease:

1. New Number – Original Number

2. The result ÷ Original Number × 100

☑ Or use this formula: Percent of change = $\frac{new\ number - original\ number}{original\ number} \times 100$

☑ Note: If your answer is a negative number, then this is a percentage decrease. If it is positive, then this is a percentage increase.

## Examples:

1) The price of a shirt increases from $20 to $30. What is the percentage increase?
   **Solution:** First, find the difference: $30 - 20 = 10$
   Then: $10 \div 20 \times 100 = \frac{10}{20} \times 100 = 50$. The percentage increase is 50. It means that the price of the shirt increased by 50%.

2) The price of a table increased from $25 to $40. What is the percent of increase?
   **Solution:** Use percentage formula: $Percent\ of\ change = \frac{new\ number - original\ number}{original\ number} \times$
   $100 = \frac{40 - 25}{25} \times 100 = \frac{15}{25} \times 100 = 0.6 \times 100 = 60$. The percentage increase is 60. It means that the price of the table increased by 60%.

3) The population of a town was 50,000 in the 2000 census and 40,000 in the 2010 census. By what percent did the population decrease?
   **Solution:** Use percentage formula:
   $Percent\ of\ change = \frac{new\ number - original\ number}{original\ number} \times 100 = \frac{40,000 - 50,000}{50,000} \times 100 = \frac{-10,000}{50,000} \times$
   $100 = -0.2 \times 100 = -20$. The population of the town decreased by 20%.

# Discount, Tax and Tip

☑ To find the discount: Multiply the regular price by the rate of discount

☑ To find the selling price: Original price – discount

☑ To find the tax: Multiply the tax rate to the taxable amount (income, property value, etc.)

☑ To find tip, multiply the rate to the selling price.

## Examples:

1) With an 10% discount, Ella saved $45 on a dress. What was the original price of the dress?

   **Solution:** let $x$ be the original price of the dress. Then: $10 \% \text{ of } x = 45$. Write an equation and solve for $x$: $0.10 \times x = 45 \rightarrow x = \frac{45}{0.10} = 450$. The original price of the dress was $450.

2) Sophia purchased a new computer for a price of $950 at the Apple Store. What is the total amount her credit card is charged if the sales tax is 7%?

   **Solution:** The taxable amount is $950, and the tax rate is 7%. Then: $Tax = 0.07 \times 950 = 66.50$

   $Final\ price = Selling\ price + Tax \rightarrow final\ price = \$950 + \$66.50 = \$1,016.50$

3) Nicole and her friends went out to eat at a restaurant. If their bill was $80.00 and they gave their server a 15% tip, how much did they pay altogether?

   **Solution:** First, find the tip. To find the tip, multiply the rate to the bill amount.

   $Tip = 80 \times 0.15 = 12$. The final price is: $\$80 + \$12 = \$92$

# Simple Interest

- ✓ Simple Interest: The charge for borrowing money or the return for lending it.

- ✓ Simple interest is calculated on the initial amount (principal).

- ✓ To solve a simple interest problem, use this formula:

  Interest = principal × rate × time $\quad (I = p \times r \times t = prt)$

## Examples:

1) Find simple interest for $300 investment at 6% for 5 years.

   **Solution:** Use Interest formula: $I = prt$ ($P = \$300$, r $= 6\% = \frac{6}{100} = 0.06$ and $t = 5$)
   Then: $I = 300 \times 0.06 \times 5 = \$90$

2) Find simple interest for $1,600 at 5% for 2 years.

   **Solution:** Use Interest formula: $I = prt$ ($P = \$1,600$, r $= 5\% = \frac{5}{100} = 0.05$ and $t = 2$)
   Then: $I = 1,600 \times 0.05 \times 2 = \$160$

3) Andy received a student loan to pay for his educational expenses this year. What is the interest on the loan if he borrowed $6,500 at 8% for 6 years?
   **Solution:** Use Interest formula: $I = prt$. $P = \$6,500$, r $= 8\% = 0.08$ and $t = 6$

   Then: $I = 6,500 \times 0.08 \times 8 = \$3,120$

4) Bob is starting his own small business. He borrowed $10,000 from the bank at a 6% rate for 6 months. Find the interest Bob will pay on this loan.
   **Solution:** Use Interest formula: $I = prt$. $P = \$10,000$, r $= 6\% = 0.06$ and $t = 0.5$ (6 months is half year). Then: $I = 10,000 \times 0.06 \times 0.5 = \$300$

# Chapter 5: Practices

✍ *Solve each problem.*

1) 15 is what percent of 60? _25_ %

2) 18 is what percent of 24? ____ %

3) 25 is what percent of 500? ____ %

4) 14 is what percent of 280? ____ %

5) 45 is what percent of 180? ____ %

6) 70 is what percent of 350? _20_ %

✍ *Solve each percent of change problem.*

7) Bob got a raise, and his hourly wage increased from $15 to $18. What is the percent increase? _____ %

8) The price of a pair of shoes increases from $40 to $66. What is the percent increase? ____ %

9) At a coffeeshop, the price of a cup of coffee increased from $1.20 to $1.44. What is the percent increase in the cost of the coffee? _20_ %

✍ *Find the selling price of each item.*

10) Original price of a computer: $650

Tax: 8%, Selling price: $_____

11) Original price of a laptop: $480

Tax: 15%, Selling price: $_552_

12) Nicolas hired a moving company. The company charged $400 for its services, and Nicolas gives the movers a 15% tip. How much does Nicolas tip the movers? $_____

13) Mason has lunch at a restaurant and the cost of his meal is $30. Mason wants to leave a 20% tip. What is Mason's total bill including tip? $_____

44                                    **ALEKS Mathematics Prep 2020-2021**

✎ *Determine the simple interest for these loans.*

14) $440 at 5% for 6 years. $ 132

15) $460 at 2.5% for 4 years. $__

16) $500 at 3% for 5 years. $__

17) $550 at 9% for 2 years. $__

18) A new car, valued at $28,000, depreciates at 9% per year. What is the value of the car one year after purchase? $_____

19) Sara puts $4,000 into an investment yielding 5% annual simple interest; she left the money in for five years. How much interest does Sara get at the end of those five years? $ 1,000

# Answers – Chapter 5

1) 25%
2) 75%
3) 5%
4) 5%
5) 25%
6) 20%
7) 20%
8) 65%
9) 20%
10) $702.00

11) $552.00
12) $60.00
13) $36.00
14) $132
15) $46
16) $75
17) $99
18) $25,480.00
19) $1,000.00

# Chapter 6:

# Expressions and Variables

---

**Math topics that you'll learn in this chapter:**

- ✓ Simplifying Variable Expressions

- ✓ Simplifying Polynomial Expressions

- ✓ The Distributive Property

- ✓ Evaluating One Variable

- ✓ Evaluating Two Variables

# Simplifying Variable Expressions

- ☑ In algebra, a variable is a letter used to stand for a number. The most common letters are: $x, y, z, a, b, c, m, and\ n$.
- ☑ An algebraic expression is an expression that contains integers, variables, and math operations such as addition, subtraction, multiplication, division, etc.
- ☑ In an expression, we can combine "like" terms. (values with same variable and same power)

## Examples:

1) Simplify. $(2x + 3x + 4) =$

   **Solution:** In this expression, there are three terms: $2x, 3x$, and 4. Two terms are "like terms": $2x$ and $3x$. Combine like terms. $2x + 3x = 5x$. Then: $(2x + 3x + 4) = 5x + 4$ (remember you cannot combine variables and numbers.)

2) Simplify. $12 - 3x^2 + 5x + 4x^2 =$

   **Solution:** Combine "like" terms: $-3x^2 + 4x^2 = x^2$. Then:

   $12 - 3x^2 + 5x + 4x^2 = 12 + x^2 + 5x$. Write in standard form (biggest powers first): $12 + x^2 + 5x = x^2 + 5x + 12$

3) Simplify. $(10x^2 + 2x^2 + 3x) =$

   **Solution:** Combine like terms. Then: $(10x^2 + 2x^2 + 3x) = 12x^2 + 3x$

4) Simplify. $15x - 3x^2 + 9x + 5x^2 =$

   **Solution:** Combine "like" terms: $15x + 9x = 24x$, and $-3x^2 + 5x^2 = 2x^2$

   Then: $15x - 3x^2 + 9x + 5x^2 = 24x + 2x^2$. Write in standard form (biggest powers first): $24x + 2x^2 = 2x^2 + 24x$

# Simplifying Polynomial Expressions

☑ In mathematics, a polynomial is an expression consisting of variables and coefficients that involves only the operations of addition, subtraction, multiplication, and non-negative integer exponents of variables. $P(x) = a_n x^n + a_{n-1} x^{n-1} + \ldots + a_2 x^2 + a_1 x + a_0$

☑ Polynomials must always be simplified as much as possible. It means you must add together any like terms. (values with same variable and same power)

## Examples:

1) **Simplify this Polynomial Expressions.** $x^2 - 5x^3 + 2x^4 - 4x^3$

   **Solution:** Combine "like" terms: $-5x^3 - 4x^3 = -9x^3$

   Then: $x^2 - 5x^3 + 2x^4 - 4x^3 = x^2 - 9x^3 + 2x^4$

   Now, write the expression in standard form: $2x^4 - 9x^3 + x^2$

2) **Simplify this expression.** $(2x^2 - x^3) - (x^3 - 4x^2) =$

   **Solution:** First, use distributive property: $\rightarrow$ multiply $(-)$ into $(x^3 - 4x^2)$

   $(2x^2 - x^3) - (x^3 - 4x^2) = 2x^2 - x^3 - x^3 + 4x^2$

   Then combine "like" terms: $2x^2 - x^3 - x^3 + 4x^2 = 6x^2 - 2x^3$

   And write in standard form: $6x^2 - 2x^3 = -2x^3 + 6x^2$

3) **Simplify.** $4x^4 - 5x^3 + 15x^4 - 12x^3 =$

   **Solution:** Combine "like" terms: $-5x^3 - 12x^3 = -17x^3$ and $4x^4 + 15x^4 = 19x^4$

   Then: $4x^4 - 5x^3 + 15x^4 - 12x^3 = 19x^4 - 17x^3$

# The Distributive Property

☑ The distributive property (or the distributive property of multiplication over addition and subtraction) simplifies and solves expressions in the form of: $a(b + c)$ or $a(b - c)$

☑ The distributive property is multiplying a term outside the parentheses by the terms inside.

☑ Distributive Property rule: $a(b + c) = ab + ac$

## Examples:

1) **Simply using distributive property.** $(-4)(x - 5)$

   **Solution:** Use the Distributive Property rule: $a(b + c) = ab + ac$

   $(-4)(x - 5) = (-4 \times x) + (-4) \times (-5) = -4x + 20$

2) **Simply.** $(3)(2x - 4)$

   **Solution:** Use Distributive Property rule: $a(b + c) = ab + ac$

   $(3)(2x - 4) = (3 \times 2x) + (3) \times (-4) = 6x - 12$

3) **Simply.** $(-3)(3x - 5) + 4x$

   **Solution:** First, simplify $(-3)(3x - 5)$ using the distributive property.

   Then: $(-3)(3x - 5) = -9x + 15$

   Now combine like terms: $(-3)(3x - 5) + 4x = -9x + 15 + 4x$

   In this expression, $-9x$ and $4x$ are "like terms" and we can combine them.

   $-9x + 4x = -5x$. Then: $-9x + 15 + 4x = -5x + 15$

# Evaluating One Variable

☑ To evaluate one variable expression, find the variable and substitute a number for that variable.

☑ Perform the arithmetic operations.

## Examples:

1) **Calculate this expression for** $x = 3$.      $15 - 3x$

   **Solution:** First, substitute 3 for $x$

   Then: $15 - 3x = 15 - 3(3)$

   Now, use order of operation to find the answer: $15 - 3(3) = 15 - 9 = 6$

2) **Evaluate this expression for** $x = 1$.      $5x - 12$

   **Solution:** First, substitute 1 for $x$, then:

   $5x - 12 = 5(1) - 12$

   Now, use order of operation to find the answer: $5(1) - 12 = 5 - 12 = -7$

3) **Find the value of this expression when** $x = 5$. $25 - 4x$

   **Solution:** First, substitute 5 for $x$, then:

   $25 - 4x = 25 - 4(5) = 25 - 20 = 5$

4) **Solve this expression for** $x = -2$.    $12 + 3x$

   **Solution:** Substitute $-2$ for $x$, then: $12 + 3x = 12 + 3(-2) = 12 - 6 = 6$

# Evaluating Two Variables

☑ To evaluate an algebraic expression, substitute a number for each variable.

☑ Perform the arithmetic operations to find the value of the expression.

## Examples:

1) **Calculate this expression for** $a = 3$ **and** $b = -2$. $3a - 6b$

   **Solution:** First, substitute 3 for $a$, and $-2$ for $b$, then:
   $$3a - 6b = 3(3) - 6(-2)$$
   Now, use order of operation to find the answer: $3(3) - 6(-2) = 9 + 12 = 21$

2) **Evaluate this expression for** $x = 3$ **and** $y = 1$. $3x + 5y$

   **Solution:** Substitute 3 for $x$, and 1 for $y$, then:
   $$3x + 5y = 3(3) + 5(1) = 9 + 5 = 14$$

3) **Find the value of this expression when** $a = 1$ **and** $b = 2$. $5(3a - 2b)$

   **Solution:** Substitute 1 for $a$, and 2 for $b$, then:
   $$5(3a - 2b) = 15a - 10b = 15(1) - 10(2) = 15 - 20 = -5$$

4) **Solve this expression.** $4x - 3y$, $x = 3$, $y = 5$

   **Solution:** Substitute 3 for $x$, and 5 for $y$ and simplify. Then: $4x - 3y = 4(3) - 3(5) = 12 - 15 = -3$

# Chapter 6: Practices

✍ *Simplify each expression.*

1) $(6x - 4x + 8 + 6) =$ $2x + 14$

2) $(-14x + 26x - 12) =$

3) $(24x - 6 - 18x + 3) =$

4) $5 + 8x^2 - 9 =$

5) $7x - 4x^2 + 6x =$

6) $15x^2 - 3x - 6x^2 + 4 =$

✍ *Simplify each polynomial.*

7) $2x^2 + 5x^3 - 7x^2 + 12x =$ $5x^3 + 5x^2 + 12x$

8) $2x^4 - 5x^5 + 8x^4 - 8x^2 =$ _____

9) $5x^3 + 15x - x^2 - 2x^3 =$ _____

10) $(8x^3 - 6x^2) + (9x^2 - 10x) =$ _____

11) $(12x^4 + 4x^3) - (8x^3 - 2x^4) =$ _____

12) $(9x^5 - 7x^3) - (5x^3 + x^2) =$ _____

✍ *Use the distributive property to simply each expression.*

13) $4(5 + 6x) =$

14) $5(8 - 4x) =$

15) $(-6)(2 - 9x) =$

16) $(-7)(6x - 4) =$

17) $(3x + 12)4 =$

18) $(8x - 5)(-3) =$ $-24x + 15$

✍ *Evaluate each expression using the value given.*

19) $8 - x, x = -3$

20) $x + 12, x = -6$

21) $5x - 3, x = 2$

22) $4 - 6x, x = 1$  $-2$

23) $3x + 1, x = -2$

24) $15 - 2x, x = 5$

✑ *Evaluate each expression using the values given.*

25) $4x - 2y, \ x = 4, y = -2$

26) $6a + 3b, \ a = 2, b = 4$

27) $12x - 5y - 8, \ x = 2, y = 3$

28) $-7a + 3b + 9, \ a = 4, b = 6$

29) $2x + 14 + 4y, \ x = 6, y = 8$

30) $4a - (5a - b) + 5, a = 4, b = 6$

# Answers – Chapter 6

1) $2x + 14$
2) $12x - 12$
3) $6x - 3$
4) $8x^2 - 4$
5) $-4x^2 + 13x$
6) $9x^2 - 3x + 4$

7) $5x^3 - 5x^2 + 12x$
8) $-5x^5 + 10x^4 - 8x^2$
9) $3x^3 - x^2 + 15x$

10) $8x^3 + 3x^2 - 10x$
11) $14x^4 - 4x^3$
12) $9x^5 - 12x^3 - x^2$

13) $24x + 20$
14) $-20x + 40$
15) $54x - 12$
16) $-42x + 28$
17) $12x + 48$
18) $-24x + 15$

19) $11$
20) $6$
21) $7$
22) $-2$
23) $-5$
24) $5$

25) $20$
26) $24$
27) $1$
28) $-1$
29) $58$
30) $7$

# Chapter 7:

# Equations and Inequalities

---

**Math topics that you'll learn in this chapter:**

- ✓ One–Step Equations

- ✓ Multi–Step Equations

- ✓ System of Equations

- ✓ Graphing Single–Variable Inequalities

- ✓ One–Step Inequalities

- ✓ Multi–Step Inequalities

# One–Step Equations

☑ The values of two expressions on both sides of an equation are equal. Example: $ax = b$. In this equation, $ax$ is equal to $b$.

☑ Solving an equation means finding the value of the variable.

☑ You only need to perform one Math operation to solve the one-step equations.

☑ To solve a one-step equation, find the inverse (opposite) operation is being performed.

☑ The inverse operations are:

- Addition and subtraction
- Multiplication and division

## Examples:

1) **Solve this equation for** $x$. $3x = 18, x = ?$

   **Solution:** Here, the operation is multiplication (variable $x$ is multiplied by 3) and its inverse operation is division. To solve this equation, divide both sides of equation by 3:

   $$3x = 18 \rightarrow \frac{3x}{3} = \frac{18}{3} \rightarrow x = 6$$

2) **Solve this equation.** $x + 15 = 0$, $x = ?$

   **Solution:** In this equation 15 is added to the variable $x$. The inverse operation of addition is subtraction. To solve this equation, subtract 15 from both sides of the equation: $x + 15 - 15 = 0 - 15$. Then simplify: $x + 15 - 15 = 0 - 15 \rightarrow x = -15$

3) **Solve this equation for** $x$. $x - 23 = 0$

   **Solution:** Here, the operation is subtraction and its inverse operation is addition. To solve this equation, add 23 to both sides of the equation: $x + 23 - 23 = 0 - 23 \rightarrow x = -23$

# Multi–Step Equations

☑ To solve a multi-step equation, combine "like" terms on one side.

☑ Bring variables to one side by adding or subtracting.

☑ Simplify using the inverse of addition or subtraction.

☑ Simplify further by using the inverse of multiplication or division.

☑ Check your solution by plugging the value of the variable into the original equation.

## Examples:

1) **Solve this equation for** $x$. $3x + 6 = 16 - 2x$

   **Solution:** First, bring variables to one side by adding $2x$ to both sides. Then:

   $3x + 6 = 16 - 2x \rightarrow 3x + 6 + 2x = 16 - 2x + 2x$. Simplify: $5x + 6 = 16$

   Now, subtract 6 from both sides of the equation: $5x + 6 - 6 = 16 - 6 \rightarrow 5x = 10 \rightarrow$

   Divide both sides by 5: $5x = 10 \rightarrow \frac{5x}{5} = \frac{10}{5} \rightarrow x = 2$

   Let's check this solution by substituting the value of 2 for $x$ in the original equation:

   $x = 2 \rightarrow 3x + 6 = 16 - 2x \rightarrow 3(2) + 6 = 16 - 2(2) \rightarrow 6 + 6 = 16 - 4 \rightarrow 12 = 12$

   The answer $x = 2$ is correct.

2) **Solve this equation for** $x$. $-4x + 4 = 16$

   **Solution:** Subtract 4 from both sides of the equation. $-4x + 4 - 4 = 16 - 4 \rightarrow -4x = 12$

   Divide both sides by $-4$, then: $-4x = 12 \rightarrow \frac{-4x}{-4} = \frac{12}{-4} \rightarrow x = -3$

   Now, check the solution: $x = -3 \rightarrow -4x + 4 = 16 \rightarrow -4(-3) + 4 = 16 \rightarrow 16 = 16$

   The answer $x = -2$ is correct.

# System of Equations

☑ A system of equations contains two equations and two variables. For example, consider the system of equations: $x - y = 1, x + y = 5$

☑ The easiest way to solve a system of equations is using the elimination method. The elimination method uses the addition property of equality. You can add the same value to each side of an equation.

☑ For the first equation above, you can add $x + y$ to the left side and 5 to the right side of the first equation: $x - y + (x + y) = 1 + 5$. Now, if you simplify, you get: $x - y + (x + y) = 1 + 5 \rightarrow 2x = 6 \rightarrow x = 3$. Now, substitute 3 for the $x$ in the first equation: $3 - y = 1$. By solving this equation, $y = 2$

## Example:

**What is the value of** $x + y$ **in this system of equations?** $\begin{cases} x + 2y = 6 \\ 2x - y = -8 \end{cases}$

**Solution:** Solving a System of Equations by Elimination:

Multiply the first equation by $(-2)$, then add it to the second equation.

$$\begin{array}{c} -2(x + 2y = 6) \\ 2x - y = -8 \end{array} \Rightarrow \begin{array}{c} -2x - 4y = -12 \\ 2x - y = -8 \end{array} \Rightarrow -5y = -20 \Rightarrow y = 4$$

Plug in the value of $y$ into one of the equations and solve for $x$.

$x + 2(4) = 6 \Rightarrow x + 8 = 6 \Rightarrow x = 6 - 8 \Rightarrow x = -2$

Thus, $x + y = -2 + 4 = 2$

# Graphing Single–Variable Inequalities

☑ An inequality compares two expressions using an inequality sign.

☑ Inequality signs are: "less than" <, "greater than" >, "less than or equal to" ≤, and "greater than or equal to" ≥.

☑ To graph a single-variable inequality, find the value of the inequality on the number line.

☑ For less than (<) or greater than (>) draw an open circle on the value of the variable. If there is an equal sign too, then use a filled circle.

☑ Draw an arrow to the right for greater or to the left for less than.

## Examples:

**1) Draw a graph for this inequality.** $x > 3$

**Solution:** Since, the variable is greater than 3, then we need to find 3 in the number line and draw an open circle on it.

Then, draw an arrow to the right.

**2) Graph this inequality.** $x \leq -4$.

**Solution:** Since the variable is less than or equal to $-4$, then we need to find $-4$ in the number line and draw a filled circle on it. Then, draw an arrow to the left.

# One–Step Inequalities

☑ An inequality compares two expressions using an inequality sign.

☑ Inequality signs are: "less than" $<$, "greater than" $>$, "less than or equal to" $\leq$, and "greater than or equal to" $\geq$.

☑ You only need to perform one Math operation to solve the one-step inequalities.

☑ To solve one-step inequalities, find the inverse (opposite) operation is being performed.

☑ For dividing or multiplying both sides by negative numbers, flip the direction of the inequality sign.

## Examples:

**1) Solve this inequality for** x. $x + 3 \geq 4$

**Solution:** The inverse (opposite) operation of addition is subtraction. In this inequality, 3 is added to x. *To isolate* x *we need to* subtract 3 from both sides of the inequality. Then:

$x + 3 \geq 4 \to x + 3 - 3 \geq 4 - 3 \to x \geq 1$. The solution is: $x \geq 1$

**2) Solve the inequality.** $x - 5 > -4$.

**Solution:** 5 is subtracted from $x$. Add 5 to both sides. $x - 5 > -4 \to x - 5 + 5 > -4 + 5 \to x > 1$

**3) Solve.** $2x \leq -4$.

**Solution:** 2 is multiplied to $x$. Divide both sides by 2. Then: $2x \leq -4 \to \frac{2x}{2} \leq \frac{-4}{2} \to x \leq -2$

**4) Solve.** $-6x \leq 12$.

**Solution:** $-6$ is multiplied to $x$. Divide both sides by $-6$. Remember when dividing or multiplying both sides of an inequality by negative numbers, flip the direction of the inequality sign. Then:

$$-6x \leq 12 \to \frac{-6x}{-6} \geq \frac{12}{-6} \to x \geq -2$$

# Multi–Step Inequalities

✅ To solve a multi-step inequality, combine "like" terms on one side.

✅ Bring variables to one side by adding or subtracting.

✅ Isolate the variable.

✅ Simplify using the inverse of addition or subtraction.

✅ Simplify further by using the inverse of multiplication or division.

✅ For dividing or multiplying both sides by negative numbers, flip the direction of the inequality sign.

## Examples:

1) **Solve this inequality.** $2x - 3 \leq 5$

   **Solution:** In this inequality, 3 is subtracted from $2x$. The inverse of subtraction is addition. Add 3 to both sides of the inequality: $2x - 3 + 3 \leq 5 + 3 \rightarrow 2x \leq 8$

   Now, divide both sides by 2. Then: $2x \leq 8 \rightarrow \frac{2x}{2} \leq \frac{8}{2} \rightarrow x \leq 4$

   The solution of this inequality is $x \leq 4$.

2) **Solve this inequality.** $3x + 9 < 12$

   **Solution:** First, subtract 9 from both sides: $3x + 9 - 9 < 12 - 9$

   Then simplify: $3x + 9 - 9 < 12 - 9 \rightarrow 3x < 3$

   Now divide both sides by 3: $\frac{3x}{3} < \frac{3}{3} \rightarrow x < 1$

3) **Solve this inequality.** $-2x + 4 \geq 6$

   First, subtract 4 from both sides: $-2x + 4 - 4 \geq 6 - 4 \rightarrow -2x \geq 2$

   Divide both sides by $-2$. Remember that you need to flip the direction of inequality sign.

   $$-2x \geq 2 \rightarrow \frac{-2x}{-2} \leq \frac{2}{-2} \rightarrow x \leq -1$$

# Chapter 7: Practices

✎ **Solve each equation. (One–Step Equations)**

1) $x + 7 = 6, x =$ ____

2) $8 = 2 - x, x =$ ____

3) $-10 = 8 + x, x =$ ____

4) $x - 5 = -1, x =$ ____

5) $16 = x + 9, x =$ ____

6) $12 - x = -5, x =$ ____

✎ **Solve each equation. (Multi–Step Equations)**

7) $5(x + 3) = 20$

8) $-4(7 - x) = 16$

9) $8 = -2(x + 5)$

10) $14 = 3(4 - 2x)$

11) $5(x + 7) = -10$

12) $-2(6 + 3x) = 12$

✎ **Solve each system of equations.**

13) $-5x + y = -3$    $x =$
     $3x - 8y = 24$    $y =$

14) $3x - 2y = 2$    $x =$
     $x - y = 2$    $y =$

15) $4x + 7y = 2$    $x =$
     $6x + 7y = 10$    $y = -2$

16) $5x + 7y = 18$    $x =$
     $-3x + 7y = -22$    $y =$

✎ **Draw a graph for each inequality.**

17) $x \leq -2$

18) $x > -6$

✎ *Solve each inequality and graph it.*

19) $x - 3 \geq -1$

20) $3x - 2 < 16$

✎ *Solve each inequality.*

21) $3x + 15 > -6$

22) $-18 + 4x \leq 10$

23) $4(x + 5) \geq 8$

24) $7x - 16 < 12$

25) $3(9 + x) \geq 15$

26) $-8 + 6x > 22$

**ALEKS Mathematics Prep 2020-2021**

# Answers – Chapter 7

1) $-1$

2) $-6$

3) $-18$

4) $4$

5) $7$

6) $17$

7) $1$

8) $11$

9) $-9$

10) $-\dfrac{1}{3}$

11) $-9$

12) $-4$

13) $x = 0$, $y = -3$

14) $x = -2$, $y = -4$

15) $x = 4$, $y = -2$

16) $x = 5$, $y = -1$

17)

18)

19)

20)

21) $x > -7$

22) $x \leq 7$

23) $x \geq -3$

24) $x < 4$

25) $x \geq -4$

26) $x > 5$

# Chapter 8:

# Lines and Slope

**Math topics that you'll learn in this chapter:**

- ✓ Finding Slope

- ✓ Graphing Lines Using Slope–Intercept Form

- ✓ Writing Linear Equations

- ✓ Graphing Linear Inequalities

- ✓ Finding Midpoint

- ✓ Finding Distance of Two Points

# Finding Slope

☑ The slope of a line represents the direction of a line on the coordinate plane.

☑ A coordinate plane contains two perpendicular number lines. The horizontal line is $x$ and the vertical line is $y$. The point at which the two axes intersect is called the origin. An ordered pair $(x, y)$ shows the location of a point.

☑ A line on a coordinate plane can be drawn by connecting two points.

☑ To find the slope of a line, we need the equation of the line or two points on the line.

☑ The slope of a line with two points A $(x_1, y_1)$ and B $(x_2, y_2)$ can be found by using this formula: $\frac{y_2 - y_1}{x_2 - x_1} = \frac{rise}{run}$

☑ The equation of a line is typically written as $y = mx + b$ where $m$ is the slope and $b$ is the $y$-intercept.

## Examples:

1) **Find the slope of the line through these two points:** $A(2, -7)$ and $B(4, 3)$.

   **Solution:** Slope $= \frac{y_2 - y_1}{x_2 - x_1}$. Let $(x_1, y_1)$ be $A(2, -7)$ and $(x_2, y_2)$ be $B(4, 3)$. (Remember, you can choose any point for $(x_1, y_1)$ and $(x_2, y_2)$). *Then:* slope $= \frac{y_2 - y_1}{x_2 - x_1} = \frac{3 - (-7)}{4 - 2} = \frac{10}{2} = 5$

   The slope of the line through these two points is 5.

2) **Find the slope of the line with equation** $y = 3x + 6$

   **Solution:** when the equation of a line is written in the form of $y = mx + b$, the slope is $m$. In this line: $y = 3x + 6$, the slope is 3.

# Graphing Lines Using Slope–Intercept Form

☑ Slope-intercept form of a line: given the slope $m$ and the $y$-intercept (the intersection of the line and y-axis) $b$, then the equation of the line is: $y = mx + b$

☑ To draw the graph of a linear equation in a slope-intercept form on the $xy$ coordinate plane, find two points on the line by plugging two values for $x$ and calculating the values of $y$.

☑ You can also use the slope ($m$) and one point to graph the line.

## Example:

1) **Sketch the graph of** $y = 2x - 4$.

**Solution:** To graph this line, we need to find two points. When $x$ is zero the value of $y$ is $-4$. And when $x$ is 2 the value of $y$ is 0.

$$x = 0 \rightarrow y = 2(0) - 4 = -4,$$
$$y = 0 \rightarrow 0 = 2x - 4 \rightarrow x = 2$$

Now, we have two points: $(0, -4)$ and $(2, 0)$.

Find the points on the coordinate plane and graph the line. Remember that the slope of the line is 2.

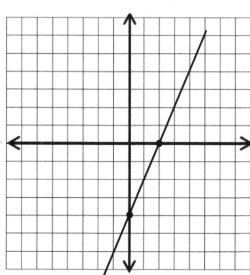

# Writing Linear Equations

☑ The equation of a line in slope-intercept form: $y = mx + b$

☑ To write the equation of a line, first identify the slope.

☑ Find the y-intercept. This can be done by substituting the slope and the coordinates of a point $(x, y)$ on the line.

## Examples:

1) What is the equation of the line that passes through $(2, -4)$ and has a slope of $8$?

   **Solution:** The general slope-intercept form of the equation of a line is $y = mx + b$, where $m$ is the slope and $b$ is the $y$-intercept.

   By substitution of the given point and given slope: $y = mx + b \rightarrow -4 = (2)(8) + b$

   So, $b = -4 - 16 = -20$, and the required equation is $y = 8x - 20$

2) Write the equation of the line through two points $A(2, 1)$ and $B(-2, 5)$.

   **Solution:** Fist, find the slope: $Slop = \frac{y_2 - y_1}{x_2 - x_1} = \frac{5 - 1}{-2 - 2} = \frac{4}{-4} = -1 \rightarrow m = -1$

   To find the value of $b$, use either points and plug in the values of $x$ and $y$ in the equation. The answer will be the same: $y = -x + b$. Let's check both points. Then:

   $(2, 1) \rightarrow y = mx + b \rightarrow 1 = -1(2) + b \rightarrow b = 3$

   $(-2, 5) \rightarrow y = mx + b \rightarrow 5 = -1(-2) + b \rightarrow b = 3$. The y-intercept of the line is 3.

   The equation of the line is: $y = -x + 3$

3) What is the equation of the line that passes through $(2, -1)$ and has a slope of $5$?

   **Solution:** The general slope-intercept form of the equation of a line is $y = mx + b$, where $m$ is the slope and $b$ is the $y$-intercept.

   By substitution of the given point and given slope: $y = mx + b \rightarrow -1 = (5)(2) + b$

   So, $b = -1 - 10 = -11$, and the equation of the line is: $y = 5x - 11$.

# Finding Midpoint

- ✓ The middle of a line segment is its midpoint.

- ✓ The Midpoint of two endpoints A $(x_1, y_1)$ and B $(x_2, y_2)$ can be found using this formula: $M\left(\frac{x_1+x_2}{2}, \frac{y_1+y_2}{2}\right)$

## Examples:

1) Find the midpoint of the line segment with the given endpoints. $(1, -3), (3, 7)$

   **Solution:** Midpoint = $\left(\frac{x_1+x_2}{2}, \frac{y_1+y_2}{2}\right) \rightarrow (x_1, y_1) = (1, -3)$ and $(x_2, y_2) = (3, 7)$

   Midpoint = $\left(\frac{1+3}{2}, \frac{-3+7}{2}\right) \rightarrow \left(\frac{4}{2}, \frac{4}{2}\right) \rightarrow M(2, 2)$

2) Find the midpoint of the line segment with the given endpoints. $(-4, 5), (8, -7)$

   **Solution:** Midpoint = $\left(\frac{x_1+x_2}{2}, \frac{y_1+y_2}{2}\right) \rightarrow (x_1, y_1) = (-4, 5)$ and $(x_2, y_2) = (8, -7)$

   Midpoint = $\left(\frac{-4+8}{2}, \frac{5-7}{2}\right) \rightarrow \left(\frac{4}{2}, \frac{-2}{2}\right) \rightarrow M(2, -1)$

3) Find the midpoint of the line segment with the given endpoints. $(5, -2), (1, 10)$

   **Solution:** Midpoint = $\left(\frac{x_1+x_2}{2}, \frac{y_1+y_2}{2}\right) \rightarrow (x_1, y_1) = (5, -2)$ and $(x_2, y_2) = (1, 10)$

   Midpoint = $\left(\frac{5+1}{2}, \frac{-2+10}{2}\right) \rightarrow \left(\frac{6}{2}, \frac{8}{2}\right) \rightarrow M(3, 4)$

4) Find the midpoint of the line segment with the given endpoints. $(2, 3), (12, -9)$

   **Solution:** Midpoint = $\left(\frac{x_1+x_2}{2}, \frac{y_1+y_2}{2}\right) \rightarrow (x_1, y_1) = (2, 3)$ and $(x_2, y_2) = (12, -3)$

   Midpoint = $\left(\frac{2+12}{2}, \frac{3-9}{2}\right) \rightarrow \left(\frac{14}{2}, \frac{-6}{2}\right) \rightarrow M(7, -3)$

# Finding Distance of Two Points

☑ Use the following formula to find the distance of two points with the coordinates A $(x_1, y_1)$ and B $(x_2, y_2)$:

$$d = \sqrt{(x_2 - x_1)^2 + (y_2 - y_1)^2}$$

## Examples:

1) Find the distance between $(4, 6)$ *and* $(1, 2)$.

**Solution:** *Use distance of two points formula:* $d = \sqrt{(x_2 - x_1)^2 + (y_2 - y_1)^2}$

$(x_1, y_1) = (4, 6)$ and $(x_2, y_2) = (1, 2)$. *Then:* $d = \sqrt{(x_2 - x_1)^2 + (y_2 - y_1)^2} \rightarrow$

$d = \sqrt{(1 - (4))^2 + (2 - 6)^2} = \sqrt{(-3)^2 + (-4)^2} = \sqrt{9 + 16} = \sqrt{25} = 5 \rightarrow d = 5$

2) Find the distance of two points $(-6, -10)$ *and* $(-2, -10)$.

**Solution:** *Use distance of two points formula:* $d = \sqrt{(x_2 - x_1)^2 + (y_2 - y_1)^2}$

$(x_1, y_1) = (-6, -10)$, and $(x_2, y_2) = (-2, -10)$

Then: $d = \sqrt{(x_2 - x_1)^2 + (y_2 - y_1)^2} \rightarrow d = \sqrt{(-2 - (-6))^2 + (-10 - (-10))^2} =$

$\sqrt{(4)^2 + (0)^2} = \sqrt{16 + 0} = \sqrt{16} = 4$. Then: $d = 4$

3) Find the distance between $(-6, 5)$ *and* $(-2, 2)$.

**Solution:** *Use distance of two points formula:* $d = \sqrt{(x_2 - x_1)^2 + (y_2 - y_1)^2}$

$(x_1, y_1) = (-6, 5)$ and $(x_2, y_2) = (-2, 2)$. Then: $d = \sqrt{(x_2 - x_1)^2 + (y_2 - y_1)^2} \rightarrow$

$d = \sqrt{(-2 - (-6))^2 + (2 - 5)^2} = \sqrt{(4)^2 + (-3)^2} = \sqrt{16 + 9} = \sqrt{25} = 5$

# Chapter 8: Practices

✍ **Find the slope of each line.**

1) $y = x - 1$  |

2) $y = -2x + 5$  -2

3) $y = 2x - 1$  -2

4) Line through $(-2, 4)$ and $(6, 0)$

5) Line through $(-3, 5)$ and $(-2, 8)$

6) Line through $(-3, -1)$ and $(0, -4)$

$-\dfrac{1}{2}$

✍ **Sketch the graph of each line. (Using Slope–Intercept Form)**

7) $y = x + 2$

8) $y = 2x - 3$

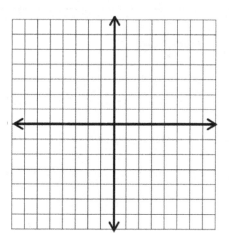

✍ **Solve.**

9) What is the equation of a line with slope 4 and intercept 12? ___ $y = 4x + 12$ ___

10) What is the equation of a line with slope 4 and passes through point $(4, 2)$?

_____

11) What is the equation of a line with slope $-2$ and passes through point $(-2, 4)$?

_____

12) The slope of a line is $-3$ and it passes through point $(-1, 5)$. What is the equation of the line? _____

13) The slope of a line is 3 and it passes through point $(-1, 4)$. What is the equation of the line? _____

ALEKS Mathematics Prep 2020-2021

✍ *Sketch the graph of each linear inequality. (Graphing Linear Inequalities)*

15) $y > 3x - 1$

16) $y < -x + 4$

✍ *Find the midpoint of the line segment with the given endpoints.*

17) $(2, 5), (-2, 7)$ 0,6

18) $(-3, 6), (5, 2)$ 1,4

19) $(9, -7), (-6, 5)$

20) $(14, -8), (-4, -2)$

21) $(-11, 2), (3, 8)$

22) $(7, 10), (1, -6)$

✍ *Find the distance between each pair of points.*

23) $(3, 10), (-2, -2)$ 5,12

24) $(1, 6), (4, 10)$ 5

25) $(-2, -1), (-8, 7)$

26) $(8, -2), (5, -6)$

27) $(4, -3), (-5, 9)$

28) $(0, 6), (3, 2)$

# Answers – Chapter 8

**Find the slope of the line through each pair of points.**

1) 1
2) −2
3) 2

4) $-\frac{1}{2}$
5) 3
6) −1

**Sketch the graph of each line. (Using Slope–Intercept Form)**

7) $y = x + 2$

8) $y = 2x - 3$

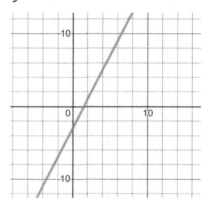

**Write the equation of the line through the given points.**

9) $y = 4x + 12$
10) $y = 4x - 14$
11) $y = -2x + 8$
12) $y = -3x + 2$
13) $y = 3x + 7$

**Sketch the graph of each linear inequality. (Graphing Linear Inequalities)**

15) $y > 3x - 1$

16) $y < -x + 4$

**Find the midpoint of the line segment with the given endpoints.**

17) $(0, 6)$

18) $(1, 4)$

19) $(1.5, -1)$

20) $(5, -5)$

21) $(-4, 5)$

22) $(4, 2)$

**Find the distance between each pair of points.**

23) 13

24) 5

25) 10

26) 5

27) 15

28) 5

# Chapter 9:

# Exponents and Variables

**Math topics that you'll learn in this chapter:**

- ✓ Multiplication Property of Exponents

- ✓ Division Property of Exponents

- ✓ Powers of Products and Quotients

- ✓ Zero and Negative Exponents

- ✓ Negative Exponents and Negative Bases

- ✓ Scientific Notation

- ✓ Radicals

# Multiplication Property of Exponents

☑ Exponents are shorthand for repeated multiplication of the same number by itself. For example, instead of $2 \times 2$, we can write $2^2$. For $3 \times 3 \times 3 \times 3$, we can write $3^4$

☑ In algebra, a variable is a letter used to stand for a number. The most common letters are: $x, y, z, a, b, c, m,$ and $n$.

☑ Exponent's rules: $x^a \times x^b = x^{a+b}$ , $\frac{x^a}{x^b} = x^{a-b}$

$$(x^a)^b = x^{a \times b} \qquad (xy)^a = x^a \times y^a \qquad \left(\frac{a}{b}\right)^c = \frac{a^c}{b^c}$$

## Examples:

1) **Multiply.** $4x^3 \times 2x^2$

   **Solution:** Use Exponent's rules: $x^a \times x^b = x^{a+b} \rightarrow x^3 \times x^2 = x^{3+2} = x^5$

   Then: $4x^3 \times 2x^2 = 8x^5$

2) **Simplify.** $(x^3 y^5)^2$

   **Solution:** Use Exponent's rules: $(x^a)^b = x^{a \times b}$. Then: $(x^3 y^5)^2 = x^{3 \times 2} y^{5 \times 2} = x^6 y^{10}$

3) **Multiply.** $-2x^5 \times 7x^3$

   **Solution:** Use Exponent's rules: $x^a \times x^b = x^{a+b} \rightarrow x^5 \times x^3 = x^{5+3} = x^8$

   Then: $-2x^5 \times 7x^3 = -14x^8$

4) **Simplify.** $(x^2 y^4)^3$

   **Solution:** Use Exponent's rules: $(x^a)^b = x^{a \times b}$. Then: $(x^2 y^4)^3 = x^{2 \times 3} y^{4 \times 3} = x^6 y^{12}$

# Division Property of Exponents

- ☑ Exponents are shorthand for repeated multiplication of the same number by itself. For example, instead of $3 \times 3$, we can write $3^2$. For $2 \times 2 \times 2$, we can write $2^3$

- ☑ For division of exponents use following formulas:

$$\frac{x^a}{x^b} = x^{a-b}, \, x \neq 0, \qquad \frac{x^a}{x^b} = \frac{1}{x^{b-a}}, \, x \neq 0, \qquad \frac{1}{x^b} = x^{-b}$$

## Examples:

1) *Simplify.* $\frac{12x^2y}{4xy^3} =$

**Solution:** First, cancel the common factor: $4 \rightarrow \frac{12x^2y}{4xy^3} = \frac{3x^2y}{xy^3}$

Use Exponent's rules: $\frac{x^a}{x^b} = x^{a-b} \rightarrow \frac{x^2}{x} = x^{2-1} = x$ and $\frac{y}{y^3} = \frac{1}{y^{3-1}} = \frac{1}{y^2}$

Then: $\frac{12x^2y}{4xy^3} = \frac{3x}{y^2}$

2) *Simplify.* $\frac{18x^6}{2x^3} =$

**Solution:** Use Exponent's rules: $\frac{x^a}{x^b} = x^{b-a} \rightarrow \frac{x^6}{x^3} = x^{6-3} = x^3$

Then: $\frac{18x^6}{2x^3} = 9x^3$

3) *Simplify.* $\frac{8x^3y}{40x^2y^3} =$

**Solution:** First, cancel the common factor: $8 \rightarrow \frac{8x^3y}{40x^2y^3} = \frac{x^3y}{5x^2y^3}$

Use Exponent's rules: $\frac{x^a}{x^b} = x^{a-b} \rightarrow \frac{x^3}{x^2} = x^{3-2} = x$

Then: $\frac{8x^3y}{40x^2y^3} = \frac{xy}{5y^3} \rightarrow$ now cancel the common factor: $y \rightarrow \frac{xy}{5y^3} = \frac{x}{5y^2}$

# Powers of Products and Quotients

☑ Exponents are shorthand for repeated multiplication of the same number by itself. For example, instead of $2 \times 2 \times 2$, we can write $2^3$. For $3 \times 3 \times 3 \times 3$, we can write $3^4$

☑ For any nonzero numbers $a$ and $b$ and any integer $x$, $(ab)^x = a^x \times b^x$ and $\left(\frac{a}{b}\right)^c = \frac{a^c}{b^c}$

## Examples:

1) **Simplify.** $(6x^2y^4)^2$

**Solution:** Use Exponent's rules: $(x^a)^b = x^{a \times b}$

$(6x^2y^4)^2 = (6)^2(x^2)^2(y^4)^2 = 36x^{2\times2}y^{4\times2} = 36x^4y^8$

2) **Simplify.** $\left(\frac{5x}{2x^2}\right)^2$

**Solution:** First, cancel the common factor: $x \rightarrow \left(\frac{5x}{2x^2}\right)^2 = \left(\frac{5}{2x}\right)^2$

Use Exponent's rules: $\left(\frac{a}{b}\right)^c = \frac{a^c}{b^c}$, Then: $\left(\frac{5}{2x}\right)^2 = \frac{5^2}{(2x)^2} = \frac{25}{4x^2}$

3) **Simplify.** $(3x^5y^4)^2$

**Solution:** Use Exponent's rules: $(x^a)^b = x^{a \times b}$

$(3x^5y^4)^2 = (3)^2(x^5)^2(y^4)^2 = 9x^{5\times2}y^{4\times2} = 9x^{10}y^8$

4) **Simplify.** $\left(\frac{2x}{3x^2}\right)^2$

**Solution:** First, cancel the common factor: $x \rightarrow \left(\frac{2x}{3x^2}\right)^2 = \left(\frac{2}{3x}\right)^2$

Use Exponent's rules: $\left(\frac{a}{b}\right)^c = \frac{a^c}{b^c}$, Then: $\left(\frac{2}{3x}\right)^2 = \frac{2^2}{(3x)^2} = \frac{4}{9x^2}$

# Zero and Negative Exponents

☑ Zero-Exponent Rule: $a^0 = 1$, this means that anything raised to the zero power is 1. For example: $(5xy)^0 = 1$

☑ A negative exponent simply means that the base is on the wrong side of the fraction line, so you need to flip the base to the other side. For instance, "$x^{-2}$" (pronounced as "ecks to the minus two") just means "$x^2$" but underneath, as in $\frac{1}{x^2}$.

## Examples:

1) **Evaluate.** $\left(\frac{2}{3}\right)^{-2} =$

   **Solution:** Use negative exponent's rule: $\left(\frac{x^a}{x^b}\right)^{-2} = \left(\frac{x^b}{x^a}\right)^2 \rightarrow \left(\frac{2}{3}\right)^{-2} = \left(\frac{3}{2}\right)^2 =$
   Then: $\left(\frac{3}{2}\right)^2 = \frac{3^2}{2^2} = \frac{9}{4}$

2) **Evaluate.** $\left(\frac{4}{5}\right)^{-3} =$

   **Solution:** Use negative exponent's rule: $\left(\frac{x^a}{x^b}\right)^{-2} = \left(\frac{x^b}{x^a}\right)^2 \rightarrow \left(\frac{4}{5}\right)^{-3} = \left(\frac{5}{4}\right)^3 =$
   Then: $\left(\frac{5}{4}\right)^3 = \frac{5^3}{4^3} = \frac{125}{64}$

3) **Evaluate.** $\left(\frac{x}{y}\right)^0 =$

   **Solution:** Use zero-exponent Rule: $a^0 = 1$
   Then: $\left(\frac{x}{y}\right)^0 = 1$

4) **Evaluate.** $\left(\frac{5}{6}\right)^{-1} =$

   **Solution:** Use negative exponent's rule: $\left(\frac{x^a}{x^b}\right)^{-2} = \left(\frac{x^b}{x^a}\right)^2 \rightarrow \left(\frac{5}{6}\right)^{-1} = \left(\frac{6}{5}\right)^1 = \frac{6}{5}$

# Negative Exponents and Negative Bases

☑ A negative exponent is the reciprocal of that number with a positive exponent. $(3)^{-2} = \frac{1}{3^2}$

☑ To simplify a negative exponent, make the power positive!

☑ The parenthesis is important! $-5^{-2}$ is not the same as $(-5)^{-2}$

$$-5^{-2} = -\frac{1}{5^2} \text{ and } (-5)^{-2} = +\frac{1}{5^2}$$

## Examples:

1) **Simplify.** $\left(\frac{5a}{6c}\right)^{-2} =$

   **Solution:** Use negative exponent's rule: $\left(\frac{x^a}{x^b}\right)^{-2} = \left(\frac{x^b}{x^a}\right)^2 \rightarrow \left(\frac{5a}{6c}\right)^{-2} = \left(\frac{6c}{5a}\right)^2$

   Now use exponent's rule: $\left(\frac{a}{b}\right)^c = \frac{a^c}{b^c} \rightarrow = \left(\frac{6c}{5a}\right)^2 = \frac{6^2c^2}{5^2a^2}$

   Then: $\frac{6^2c^2}{5^2a^2} = \frac{36c^2}{25a^2}$

2) **Simplify.** $\left(\frac{2x}{3yz}\right)^{-3} =$

   **Solution:** Use negative exponent's rule: $\left(\frac{x^a}{x^b}\right)^{-2} = \left(\frac{x^b}{x^a}\right)^2 \rightarrow \left(\frac{2x}{3yz}\right)^{-3} = \left(\frac{3yz}{2x}\right)^3$

   Now use exponent's rule: $\left(\frac{a}{b}\right)^c = \frac{a^c}{b^c} \rightarrow \left(\frac{3yz}{2x}\right)^3 = \frac{3^3y^3z^3}{2^3x^3} = \frac{27y^3z^3}{8x^3}$

3) **Simplify.** $\left(\frac{3a}{2c}\right)^{-2} =$

   **Solution:** Use negative exponent's rule: $\left(\frac{x^a}{x^b}\right)^{-2} = \left(\frac{x^b}{x^a}\right)^2 \rightarrow \left(\frac{3a}{2c}\right)^{-2} = \left(\frac{2c}{3a}\right)^2$

   Now use exponent's rule: $\left(\frac{a}{b}\right)^c = \frac{a^c}{b^c} \rightarrow = \left(\frac{2c}{3a}\right)^2 = \frac{2^2c^2}{3^2a^2}$

   Then: $\frac{2^2c^2}{3^2a^2} = \frac{4c^2}{9a^2}$

# Scientific Notation

☑ Scientific notation is used to write very big or very small numbers in decimal form.

☑ In scientific notation all numbers are written in the form of: $m \times 10^n$, where $m$ is greater than 1 and less than 10.

☑ To convert a number from scientific notation to standard form, move the decimal point to the left (if the exponent of ten is a negative number), or to the right (if the exponent is positive).

## Examples:

1) **Write** 0.00015 **in scientific notation.**

   **Solution:** First, move the decimal point to the right so you have a number between 1 and 10. That number is 1.5

   Now, determine how many places the decimal moved in step 1 by the power of 10. We moved the decimal point 4 digits to the right. Then: $10^{-4} \rightarrow$ When the decimal moved to the right, the exponent is negative. Then: $0.00015 = 1.5 \times 10^{-4}$

2) **Write** $9.5 \times 10^{-5}$ **in standard notation.**

   **Solution:** $10^{-5} \rightarrow$ When the decimal moved to the right, the exponent is negative. Then: $9.5 \times 10^{-5} = 0.000095$

3) **Write** 0.00012 **in scientific notation.**

   **Solution:** First, move the decimal point to the right so you have a number between 1 and 10. Then: $m = 1.2$

   Now, determine how many places the decimal moved in step 1 by the power of 10. $10^{-4} \rightarrow$ Then: $0.00012 = 1.2 \times 10^{-4}$

4) **Write** $8.3 \times 10^5$ **in standard notation.**

   **Solution:** $10^{-5} \rightarrow$ The exponent is positive 5. Then, move the decimal point to the right five digits. (remember $8.3 = 8.30000$)

   Then: $8.3 \times 10^5 = 830000$

# Chapter 9: Practices

✍ *Simplify and write the answer in exponential form.*

1) $3x^3 \times 5xy^2 =$ 〔$15x^4y^2$〕

2) $4x^2y \times 6x^2y^2 =$

3) $8x^3y^2 \times 2x^2y^3 =$

4) $7xy^4 \times 3x^2y =$

5) $6x^4y^5 \times 8x^3y^2 =$

6) $5x^3y^3 \times 8x^3y^3 =$ 〔$40x^6y^6$〕

✍ *Simplify. (Division Property of Exponents)*

7) $\frac{5^5 \times 5^3}{5^9 \times 5} =$ 〔$\frac{1}{25}$〕

8) $\frac{8x}{24x^2} =$

9) $\frac{15^{\ 4}}{9x^3} =$

10) $\frac{36^{\ 3}}{54^{\ 3}y^2} =$

11) $\frac{14y^3}{49x^4y^4} =$

12) $\frac{120x^3y^5}{30^{\ 2}y^3} =$

✍ *Simplify. (Powers of Products and Quotients)*

13) $(8x^4y^6)^3 =$

14) $(3x^5y^4)^6 =$ 〔$729x^{30}y^{24}$〕

15) $(5x \times 4xy^2)^2 =$

16) $(\frac{6x}{x^3})^2 =$

17) $\left(\frac{2x^3y^5}{6x^4y^2}\right)^2 =$

18) $\left(\frac{42^{\ 4}y^6}{21x^3y^5}\right)^3 =$

✎ *Evaluate these expressions. (Zero and Negative Exponents)*

19) $\left(\frac{2}{5}\right)^{-2} =$

20) $\left(\frac{1}{2}\right)^{-8} =$

21) $\left(\frac{2}{5}\right)^{-3} = \dfrac{125}{8}$

22) $\left(\frac{3}{7}\right)^{-2} =$

23) $\left(\frac{5}{6}\right)^{-3} =$

24) $\left(\frac{4}{9}\right)^{-2} =$

✎ *Simplify. (Negative Exponents and Negative Bases)*

25) $16x^{-3}y^{-4} =$

26) $-9x^2y^{-3} =$

27) $12a^{-4}b^2 =$

28) $25a^3b^{-5}c^{-1} = \dfrac{25a^3}{b^5c}$

29) $\dfrac{18y}{x^2y^{-2}} =$

30) $\dfrac{21a^{-2}b}{-14c^{-4}} =$

✎ *Write each number in scientific notation.*

31) $0.00615 =$

32) $0.000048 =$

33) $36{,}000 =$

34) $82{,}000{,}000 = 8.2 \times 10^7$

**ALEKS Mathematics Prep 2020-2021**

# Answers – Chapter 9

1) $15x^4y^2$

2) $24x^4y^3$

3) $16x^5y^5$

4) $21x^3y^5$

5) $48x^7y^7$

6) $40x^6y^6$

7) $\frac{1}{25}$

8) $\frac{1}{3x}$

9) $\frac{5}{3}x$

10) $\frac{2}{3y^3}$

11) $\frac{2}{7x^4y}$

12) $4xy^2$

13) $512x^{12}y^{18}$

14) $729x^{30}y^{24}$

15) $400x^4y^4$

16) $\frac{36}{x^4}$

17) $\frac{y^6}{9x^2}$

18) $8x^3y^3$

19) $\frac{25}{4}$

20) $256$

21) $\frac{125}{8}$

22) $\frac{49}{9}$

23) $\frac{216}{125}$

24) $\frac{81}{16}$

25) $\frac{16}{x^3y^4}$

26) $-\frac{9x^2}{y^3}$

27) $\frac{12\ ^2}{a^4}$

28) $\frac{25a^3}{b^5c}$

29) $\frac{18y^3}{x^2}$

30) $-\frac{3bc^4}{2a^2}$

31) $6.15 \times 10^{-3}$

32) $4.8 \times 10^{-5}$

33) $3.6 \times 10^4$

34) $8.2 \times 10^7$

35) $7$

36) $3$

37) $12$

38) $32$

39) $6$

40) $5\sqrt{6}$

# Chapter 10:

# Polynomials

**Math topics that you'll learn in this chapter:**

- ✓ Simplifying Polynomials
- ✓ Adding and Subtracting Polynomials
- ✓ Multiplying Monomials
- ✓ Multiplying and Dividing Monomials
- ✓ Multiplying a Polynomial and a Monomial
- ✓ Multiplying Binomials
- ✓ Factoring Trinomials

**ALEKS Mathematics Prep 2020-2021**

# Simplifying Polynomials

☑ To simplify Polynomials, find "like" terms. (they have same variables with same power).

☑ Use "FOIL". (First–Out–In–Last) for binomials:

$$(x + a)(x + b) = x^2 + (b + a)x + ab$$

☑ Add or Subtract "like" terms using order of operation.

## Examples:

1) **Simplify this expression.** $x(2x + 5) + 6x =$

   **Solution:** Use Distributive Property: $x(2x + 5) = 2x^2 + 5x$

   Now, combine like terms: $x(2x + 5) + 6x = 2x^2 + 5x + 6x = 2x^2 + 11x$

2) **Simplify this expression.** $(x + 2)(x + 3) =$

   **Solution:** First, apply the FOIL method: $(a + b)(c + d) = ac + ad + bc + bd$

   $(x + 2)(x + 3) = x^2 + 3x + 2x + 6$

   Now combine like terms: $x^2 + 3x + 2x + 6 = x^2 + 5x + 6$

3) **Simplify this expression.** $4x(2x - 3) + 6x^2 - 4x =$

   **Solution:** Use Distributive Property: $4x(2x - 3) = 8x^2 - 12x$

   Then: $4x(2x - 3) + 6x^2 - 4x = 8x^2 - 12x + 6x^2 - 4x$

   Now combine like terms: $8x^2 + 6x^2 = 14x^2$, and $-12x - 4x = -16x$

   The simplified form of the expression: $8x^2 - 12x + 6x^2 - 4x = 14x^2 - 16x$

# Adding and Subtracting Polynomials

✓ Adding polynomials is just a matter of combining like terms, with some order of operations considerations thrown in.

✓ Be careful with the minus signs, and don't confuse addition and multiplication!

✓ For subtracting polynomials, sometimes you need to use the Distributive Property: $a(b + c) = ab + ac$, $a(b - c) = ab - ac$

## Examples:

1) *Simplify the expressions.* $(x^3 - 3x^4) - (2x^4 - 5x^3) =$

   **Solution:** First, use the Distributive Property: $-(2x^4 - 5x^3) = -1(2x^4 - 5x^3) = -2x^4 + 5x^3$

   $\rightarrow (x^3 - 3x^4) - (2x^4 - 5x^3) = x^3 - 3x^4 - 2x^4 + 5x^3$

   Now combine like terms: $x^3 + 5x^3 = 6x^3$ and $-3x^4 - 2x^4 = -5x^4$

   Then: $(x^3 - 3x^4) - (2x^4 - 5x^3) = x^3 - 3x^4 - 2x^4 + 5x^3 = 6x^3 - 5x^4$

   Write the answer in standard form: $6x^3 - 5x^4 = -5x^4 + 6x^3$

2) *Add expressions.* $(2x^3 - 4) + (6x^3 - 2x^2) =$

   **Solution:** Remove parentheses: $(2x^3 - 4) + (6x^3 - 2x^2) = 2x^3 - 4 + 6x^3 - 2x^2$

   Now combine like terms: $2x^3 - 4 + 6x^3 - 2x^2 = 8x^3 - 2x^2 - 4$

3) *Simplify the expressions.* $(8x^2 - 3x^3) - (2x^2 + 5x^3) =$

   **Solution:** First, use Distributive Property: $-(2x^2 + 5x^3) = -2x^2 - 5x^3 \rightarrow$

   $(8x^2 - 3x^3) - (2x^2 + 5x^3) = 8x^2 - 3x^3 - 2x^2 - 5x^3$

   Now combine like terms and write in standard form: $8x^2 - 3x^3 - 2x^2 - 5x^3 = -8x^3 + 6x^2$

**ALEKS Mathematics Prep 2020-2021**

# Multiplying Monomials

✐ A monomial is a polynomial with just one term: Examples: $2x$ or $7y^2$.

✐ When you multiply monomials, first multiply the coefficients (a number placed before and multiplying the variable) and then multiply the variables using multiplication property of exponents.

$$x^a \times x^b = x^{a+b}$$

## Examples:

1) **Multiply expressions.** $5xy^4z^2 \times 3x^2y^5z^3$

   **Solution:** Find the same variables and use multiplication property of exponents: $x^a \times x^b = x^{a+b}$

   $x \times x^2 = x^{1+2} = x^3$ , $y^4 \times y^5 = y^{4+5} = y^9$ and $z^2 \times z^3 = z^{2+3} = z^5$

   Then, multiply coefficients and variables: $5xy^4z^2 \times 3x^2y^5z^3 = 15x^3y^9z^5$

2) **Multiply expressions.** $-2a^5b^4 \times 8a^3b^4 =$

   **Solution:** Use the multiplication property of exponents: $x^a \times x^b = x^{a+b}$

   $a^5 \times a^3 = a^{5+3} = a^8$ and $b^4 \times b^4 = b^{4+4} = b^8$

   Then: $-2a^5b^4 \times 8a^3b^4 = -16a^8b^8$

3) **Multiply.** $7xy^3z^5 \times 4x^2y^4z^3$

   **Solution:** Use the multiplication property of exponents: $x^a \times x^b = x^{a+b}$

   $x \times x^2 = x^{1+2} = x^3$, $y^3 \times y^4 = y^{3+4} = y^7$ and $z^5 \times z^3 = z^{5+3} = z^8$

   Then: $7xy^3z^5 \times 4x^2y^5z^3 = 28x^3y^7z^8$

4) **Simplify.** $(5a^6b^3)(-9a^7b^2) =$

   **Solution:** Use the multiplication property of exponents: $x^a \times x^b = x^{a+b}$

   $a^6 \times a^7 = a^{6+7} = a^{13}$ and $b^3 \times b^2 = b^{3+2} = b^5$

   Then: $(5a^6b^3) \times (-9a^6b^2) = -45a^{13}b^5$

# Multiplying and Dividing Monomials

✓ When you divide or multiply two monomials you need to divide or multiply their coefficients and then divide or multiply their variables.

✓ In case of exponents with the same base, for Division, subtract their powers, for Multiplication, add their powers.

✓ Exponent's Multiplication and Division rules:

$$x^a \times x^b = x^{a+b} , \qquad \frac{x^a}{x^b} = x^{a-b}$$

## Examples:

1) **Multiply expressions.** $(-5x^8)(4x^6) =$

**Solution:** Use multiplication property of exponents: $x^a \times x^b = x^{a+b} \rightarrow x^8 \times x^6 = x^{14}$

Then: $(-5x^5)(4x^4) = -20x^{14}$

2) **Divide expressions.** $\frac{14x^5y^4}{2xy^3} =$

**Solution:** Use division property of exponents: $\frac{x^a}{x^b} = x^{a-b} \rightarrow \frac{x^5}{x} = x^{5-1} = x^4$ and $\frac{y^4}{y^3} = y$

Then: $\frac{14x^5y^4}{2xy^3} = 7x^4y$

3) **Divide expressions.** $\frac{56a^8b^3}{8ab^3}$

**Solution:** Use division property of exponents: $\frac{x^a}{x^b} = x^{a-b} \rightarrow \frac{a^8}{a} = a^{8-1} = a^7$ and $\frac{b^3}{b^3} = 1$

Then: $\frac{56a^8b^3}{8ab^3} = 7a^7$

**ALEKS Mathematics Prep 2020-2021**

# Multiplying a Polynomial and a Monomial

☑ When multiplying monomials, use the product rule for exponents.

$$x^a \times x^b = x^{a+b}$$

☑ When multiplying a monomial by a polynomial, use the distributive property.

$$a \times (b + c) = a \times b + a \times c = ab + ac$$
$$a \times (b - c) = a \times b - a \times c = ab - ac$$

## Examples:

1) **Multiply expressions.** $5x(3x - 2)$

   **Solution:** Use Distributive Property: $5x(3x - 2) = 5x \times 3x - 5x \times (-2) = 15x^2 - 10x$

2) **Multiply expressions.** $x(2x^2 + 3y^2)$

   **Solution:** Use Distributive Property: $x(2x^2 + 3y^2) = x \times 2x^2 + x \times 3y^2 = 2x^3 + 3xy^2$

3) **Multiply.** $-4x(-5x^2 + 3x - 6)$

   **Solution:** Use Distributive Property:

   $$-4x(-5x^2 + 3x - 6) = (-4x)(-5x^2) + (-4x) \times (3x) + (-4x) \times (-6) =$$

   Now, simplify: $(-4x)(-5x^2) + (-4x) \times (3x) + (-4x) \times (-6) = 20x^3 - 12x^2 + 24x$

# Multiplying Binomials

☑ A binomial is a polynomial that is the sum or the difference of two terms, each of which is a monomial.

☑ To multiply two binomials, use the "FOIL" method. (First-Out-In-Last)

$$(x + a)(x + b) = x \times x + x \times b + a \times x + a \times b = x^2 + bx + ax + ab$$

## Examples:

1) **Multiply Binomials.** $(x + 2)(x - 4) =$

   **Solution:** Use "FOIL". (First–Out–In–Last): $(x + 2)(x - 4) = x^2 - 4x + 2x - 8$

   Then combine like terms: $x^2 - 4x + 2x - 8 = x^2 - 2x - 8$

2) **Multiply.** $(x - 5)(x - 2) =$

   **Solution:** Use "FOIL". (First–Out–In–Last): $(x - 5)(x - 2) = x^2 - 2x - 5x + 10$

   Then simplify: $x^2 - 2x - 5x + 10 = x^2 - 7x + 10$

3) **Multiply.** $(x - 3)(x + 6) =$

   **Solution:** Use "FOIL". (First–Out–In–Last): $(x - 3)(x + 6) = x^2 + 6x - 3x - 18$

   Then simplify: $x^2 + 6x - 3x - 18 = x^2 + 3x - 18$

4) **Multiply Binomials.** $(x + 8)(x + 4) =$

   **Solution:** Use "FOIL". (First–Out–In–Last): $(x + 8)(x + 4) = x^2 + 4x + 8x + 32$

   Then combine like terms: $x^2 + 4x + 8x + 32 = x^2 + 12x + 32$

# Factoring Trinomials

To factor trinomials, you can use following methods:

☑ "FOIL": $(x + a)(x + b) = x^2 + (b + a)x + ab$

☑ "Difference of Squares":

$$a^2 - b^2 = (a + b)(a - b)$$

$$a^2 + 2ab + b^2 = (a + b)(a + b)$$

$$a^2 - 2ab + b^2 = (a - b)(a - b)$$

☑ "Reverse FOIL": $x^2 + (b + a)x + ab = (x + a)(x + b)$

## Examples:

1) **Factor this trinomial.** $x^2 - 2x - 8$

**Solution:** Break the expression into groups. You need to find two numbers that their product is $-8$ and their sum is $-2$. (remember "Reverse FOIL": $x^2 + (b + a)x + ab =$ $(x + a)(x + b)$). Those two numbers are 2 and $-4$. Then:

$x^2 - 2x - 8 = (x^2 + 2x) + (-4x - 8)$

Now factor out $x$ from $x^2 + 2x : x(x + 2)$, and factor out $-4$ from $-4x - 8: -4(x + 2)$

Then: $(x^2 + 2x) + (-4x - 8) = x(x + 2) - 4(x + 2)$

Now factor out like term: $(x + 2)$. Then: $(x + 2)(x - 4)$

2) **Factor this trinomial.** $x^2 - 2x - 24$

**Solution:** Break the expression into groups: $(x^2 + 4x) + (-6x - 24)$

Now factor out $x$ from $x^2 + 4x : x(x + 4)$, and factor out $-6$ from $-6x - 24: -6(x + 4)$

Then: $(x + 4) - 6(x + 4)$, now factor out like term:

$(x = 4) \rightarrow x(x + 4) - 6(x + 4) = (x + 4)(x - 6)$

# Chapter 10: Practices

✍ *Simplify each polynomial.*

1) $4(3x + 5) =$  12x  20

2) $8(6x - 1) =$

3) $2x(7x + 4) + 2x =$

4) $5x(6x + 2) - 4x =$

5) $7x(3x - 6) + x^2 - 2 =$

6) $3x^2 - 5 - 9x(4x + 1) =$

✍ *Add or subtract polynomials.*

7) $(6x^2 + 8) + (2x^2 - 4) =$  8x² + 4

8) $(x^2 - 5x) - (3x^2 + 2x) =$

9) $(9x^3 - 4x^2) + (x^3 - 3x^2) =$

10) $(7x^3 - 3x) - (6x^3 - 5x) =$

11) $(12x^3 + x^2) + (2x^2 - 10) =$

12) $(4x^3 - 15) - (3x^3 - 7x^2) =$

✍ *Simplify each expression. (Multiplying Monomials)*

13) $5x^3 \times 6x^4 =$  30x⁷

14) $-4a^2b \times 3ab^2 =$

15) $(-7x^2yz) \times (-3xy^3z^2) =$

16) $9u^4t^2 \times (-4ut) =$

17) $12x^3z \times 3xy^2 =$

18) $-8a^2bc \times a^3b^2 =$

✍ *Simplify each expression. (Multiplying and Dividing Monomials)*

19) $(4x^3y^4)(12x^5y^2) =$  48x⁸y⁶

20) $(5x^4y^2)(8x^6y^5) =$

21) $(16x^7y^9)(3x^6y^4) =$

22) $\frac{36x^5y^3}{9x^2y} =$

23) $\frac{98\ ^{12}y^{10}}{7x^9y^7} =$

24) $\frac{225x^9y^{13}}{15\ ^6y^9} =$

✎ *Find each product. (Multiplying a Polynomial and a Monomial)*

25) $4x(6x - y) = 24x^2 - 4xy$

26) $7x(3x + 5y) =$

27) $5x(x - 8y) =$

28) $x(3x^2 + 2x - 6) =$

29) $5x(-x^2 + 7x + 4) =$

30) $6x(6x^2 - 3x - 12) =$

✎ *Find each product. (Multiplying Binomials)*

31) $(x - 3)(x + 3) = x^2 - 9$

32) $(x - 5)(x - 4) =$

33) $(x + 6)(x + 3) =$

34) $(x - 7)(x + 8) =$

35) $(x + 2)(x - 9) =$

36) $(x - 15)(x + 3) =$

✎ *Factor each trinomial.*

37) $x^2 + 4x - 12 = (x - 2)(x + 6)$

38) $x^2 + x - 20 =$

39) $x^2 + 3x - 108 =$

40) $x^2 + 12x + 32 =$

41) $x^2 - 14x + 48 =$

42) $x^2 + 2x - 35 =$

# Answers – Chapter 10

1) $12x + 20$

2) $48x - 8$

3) $14x^2 + 10x$

4) $30x^2 + 6x$

5) $22x^2 - 42x - 2$

6) $-33x^2 - 9x - 5$

7) $8x^2 + 4$

8) $-2x^2 - 7x$

9) $10x^3 - 7x^2$

10) $x^3 + 2x$

11) $12x^3 + 3x^2 - 10$

12) $x^3 + 7x^2 - 15$

13) $30x^7$

14) $-12a^3b^3$

15) $21x^3y^4z^3$

16) $-36u^5t^3$

17) $36x^4y^2z$

18) $-8a^5b^3c$

19) $48x^8y^6$

20) $40x^{10}y^7$

21) $48x^{13}y^{13}$

22) $4x^3y^2$

23) $14x^3y^3$

24) $15x^3y^4$

25) $24x^2 - 4xy$

26) $21x^2 + 35xy$

27) $5x^2 - 40xy$

28) $3x^3 + 2x^2 - 6x$

29) $-5x^3 + 35x^2 + 20x$

30) $36x^3 - 18x^2 - 72x$

31) $x^2 - 9$

32) $x^2 - 9x + 20$

33) $x^2 + 9x + 18$

34) $x^2 + x - 56$

35) $x^2 - 7x - 18$

36) $x^2 - 12x - 45$

37) $(x - 2)(x + 6)$

38) $(x + 5)(x - 4)$

39) $(x + 12)(x - 9)$

40) $(x + 8)(x + 4)$

41) $(x - 6)(x - 8)$

42) $(x + 7)(x - 5)$

# Chapter 11:

# Geometry and Solid Figures

---

**Math topics that you'll learn in this chapter:**

- ✓ The Pythagorean Theorem
- ✓ Parallel Lines and Transversal
- ✓ Triangles
- ✓ Special Right Triangles
- ✓ Polygons
- ✓ Trapezoids
- ✓ Cubes
- ✓ Rectangle Prisms
- ✓ Cylinder

# The Pythagorean Theorem

☑ You can use the Pythagorean Theorem to find a missing side in a right triangle.

☑ In any right triangle: $a^2 + b^2 = c^2$

## Examples:

1) Right triangle ABC (not shown) has two legs of lengths 6 cm (AB) and 8 cm (AC). What is the length of the hypotenuse of the triangle (side BC)?

   **Solution:** Use Pythagorean Theorem: $a^2 + b^2 = c^2$, $a = 6$, and $b = 8$

   Then: $a^2 + b^2 = c^2 \rightarrow 6^2 + 8^2 = c^2 \rightarrow 36 + 64 = c^2 \rightarrow 100 = c^2 \rightarrow c = \sqrt{100} = 10$

   The length of the hypotenuse is 10 cm.

2) Find the hypotenuse of this triangle.

   **Solution:** Use Pythagorean Theorem: $a^2 + b^2 = c^2$

   Then: $a^2 + b^2 = c^2 \rightarrow 12^2 + 5^2 = c^2 \rightarrow 144 + 25 = c^2$

   $c^2 = 169 \rightarrow c = \sqrt{169} = 13$

   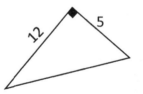

3) Find the length of the missing side in this triangle.

   **Solution:** Use Pythagorean Theorem: $a^2 + b^2 = c^2$

   Then: $a^2 + b^2 = c^2 \rightarrow 3^2 + b^2 = 5^2 \rightarrow 9 + b^2 = 25 \rightarrow$

   $b^2 = 25 - 9 \rightarrow b^2 = 16 \rightarrow b = \sqrt{16} = 4$

   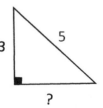

# Complementary and Supplementary angles

☑ Two angles with a sum of 90 degrees are called complementary
angles.

☑ Two angles with a sum of 180 degrees are Supplementary angles.

## Examples:

*1)* **Find the missing angle.**

**Solution***:* Notice that the two angles form a right angle. This means that
the angles are complementary, and their sum is 90. Then: $18 + x =$
$90 \rightarrow x = 90° - 18° = 72°$

The missing angle is 72 degrees. $x = 72°$

*2)* **Angles Q and S are supplementary. What is the measure of angle Q if angle
S is 35 degrees?**

**Solution***:* Q and S are supplementary $\rightarrow Q + S = 180 \rightarrow Q + 35 = 180 \rightarrow$
$$Q = 180 - 35 = 145$$

# Parallel lines and Transversals

☑ When a line (transversal) intersects two parallel lines in the same plane, eight angles are formed. In the following diagram, a transversal intersects two parallel lines. Angles 1, 3, 5, and 7 are congruent. Angles 2, 4, 6, and 8 are also congruent.

☑ In the following diagram, the following angles are supplementary angles (their sum is 180):
  - Angles 1 and 8
  - Angles 2 and 7
  - Angles 3 and 6
  - Angles 4 and 5

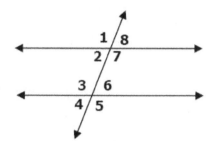

## Example:

In the following diagram, two parallel lines are cut by a transversal. What is the value of $x$?

**Solution:** The two angles $3x - 15$ and $2x + 7$ are equivalent.

That is: $3x - 15 = 2x + 7$

Now, solve for $x$:

$3x - 15 + 15 = 2x + 7 + 15$

$\rightarrow 3x = 2x + 22 \rightarrow 3x - 2x = 2x + 22 - 2x \rightarrow x = 22$

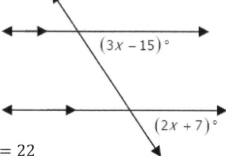

ALEKS Mathematics Prep 2020-2021

# Triangles

☑ In any triangle the sum of all angles is 180 degrees.

☑ Area of a triangle $= \frac{1}{2} (base \times height)$

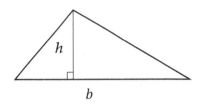

## Examples:

What is the area of the following triangles?

1)

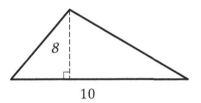

**Solution:**

Use the area formula: Area $= \frac{1}{2} (base \times height)$

$base = 10$ and $height = 8$

Area $= \frac{1}{2}(10 \times 8) = \frac{1}{2}(80) = 40$

2)

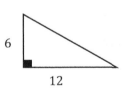

**Solution:**

Use the area formula: Area $= \frac{1}{2} (base \times height)$

$base = 12$ and $height = 6$

Area $= \frac{1}{2}(12 \times 6) = \frac{72}{2} = 36$

3) What is the missing angle in this triangle?

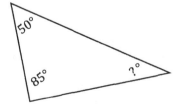

**Solution:**

In any triangle the sum of all angles is 180 degrees.

Let $x$ be the missing angle. Then: $50 + 85 + x = 180$

$\rightarrow 135 + x = 180 \rightarrow x = 180 - 135 = 45$

The missing angle is 45 degrees.

# Special Right Triangles

✓ A special right triangle is a triangle whose sides are in a particular ratio. Two special right triangles are $45° - 45° - 90°$ and $30° - 60° - 90°$ triangles.

✓ In a special $45° - 45° - 90°$ triangle, the three angles are $45°$, $45°$ and $90°$. The lengths of the sides of this triangle are in the ratio of $1 : 1 : \sqrt{2}$.

✓ In a special triangle $30° - 60° - 90°$, the three angles are $30° - 60° - 90°$. The lengths of this triangle are in the ratio of $1 : \sqrt{3} : 2$.

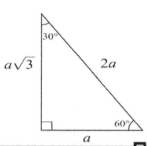

## Examples:

**1) Find the length of the hypotenuse of a right triangle if the length of the other two sides are both 4 inches.**

**Solution:** this is a right triangle with two equal sides. Therefore, it must be a $45° - 45° - 90°$ triangle. Two equivalent *sides are* 4 *inches. The ratio of sides:* $x : x : x\sqrt{2}$

The length of the hypotenuse is $4\sqrt{2}$ *inches.* $x : x : x\sqrt{2} \rightarrow 4 : 4 : 4\sqrt{2}$

**2) The length of the hypotenuse of a triangle is 6 inches. What are the lengths of the other two sides if one angle of the triangle is $30°$?**

**Solution:** The hypotenuse is 6 inches and the triangle is a $30° - 60° - 90°$ triangle.

Then, one side of the triangle is 3 (it's half the side of the hypotenuse) and the other side is $3\sqrt{3}$. (it's the smallest side times $\sqrt{3}$) $x : x\sqrt{3} : 2x \rightarrow x = 3 \rightarrow x : x\sqrt{3} : 2x = 3 : 3\sqrt{3} : 6$

ALEKS Mathematics Prep 2020-2021

# Polygons

☑ The perimeter of a square

$= 4 \times side = 4s$

☐ $s$

☑ The perimeter of a rectangle

$= 2(width + length)$

$width$

$length$

☑ The perimeter of trapezoid

$= a + b + c + d$

☑ The perimeter of a regular hexagon $= 6a$

☑ The perimeter of a parallelogram $= 2(l + w)$

---

## Examples:

1) Find the perimeter of following regular hexagon.

   **Solution:** Since the hexagon is regular, all sides are equal.

   Then: The perimeter of the hexagon $= 6 \times (one \; side)$

   The perimeter of the hexagon $= 6 \times (one \; side) = 6 \times 4 = 24 \; m$

4 m

2) Find the perimeter of following trapezoid.

   **Solution:** The perimeter of a trapezoid $= a + b + c + d$

   The perimeter of the trapezoid $= 5 + 6 + 6 + 8 = 25 \; ft$

5 ft

6 ft    6 ft

8 ft

# Trapezoids

- ☑ A quadrilateral with at least one pair of parallel sides is a trapezoid.

- ☑ Area of a trapezoid = $\frac{1}{2}h(b_1 + b_2)$

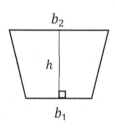

## Examples:

1)  Calculate the area of this trapezoid.

   **Solution:**

   Use area formula: $A = \frac{1}{2}h(b_1 + b_2)$

   $b_1 = 5\ cm$ , $b_2 = 8\ cm$ and $h = 10\ cm$

   Then: $A = \frac{1}{2}(10)(8 + 5) = 5(13) = 65\ cm^2$

2)  Calculate the area of this trapezoid.

   **Solution:**

   Use area formula: $A = \frac{1}{2}h(b_1 + b_2)$

   $b_1 = 12\ cm$ , $b_2 = 20\ cm$ and $h = 14\ cm$

   Then: $A = \frac{1}{2}(14)(12 + 20) = 7(32) = 224\ cm^2$

**ALEKS Mathematics Prep 2020-2021**

# Cubes

☑ A cube is a three-dimensional solid object bounded by six square sides.

☑ Volume is the measure of the amount of space inside of a solid figure, like a cube, ball, cylinder or pyramid.

☑ The volume of a cube = $(one\ side)^3$

☑ The surface area of a cube = $6 \times (one\ side)^2$

## Examples:

1) Find the volume and surface area of this cube.

**Solution:** Use volume formula: $volume = (one\ side)^3$

Then: $volume = (one\ side)^3 = (2)^3 = 8\ cm^3$

Use surface area formula: $surface\ area\ of\ cube: 6(one\ side)^2 =$
$$6(2)^2 = 6(4) = 24\ cm^2$$

2 cm

2) Find the volume and surface area of this cube.

**Solution:** Use volume formula: $volume = (one\ side)^3$

Then: $volume = (one\ side)^3 = (5)^3 = 125\ cm^3$

Use surface area formula:

$surface\ area\ of\ cube: 6(one\ side)^2 = 6(5)^2 = 6(25) = 150\ cm^2$

5 cm

3) Find the volume and surface area of this cube.

**Solution:** Use volume formula: $volume = (one\ side)^3$

Then: $volume = (one\ side)^3 = (7)^3 = 343\ m^3$

Use surface area formula:

$surface\ area\ of\ cube: 6(one\ side)^2 = 6(7)^2 = 6(49) = 294\ m^2$

7 m

# Rectangular Prisms

☑ A rectangular prism is a solid 3-dimensional object with six rectangular faces.

☑ The volume of a Rectangular prism = **Length × Width × Height**

$Volume = l \times w \times h$

$Surface\ area = 2 \times (wh + lw + lh)$

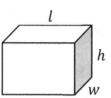

## Examples:

1) Find the volume and surface area of this rectangular prism.

   **Solution:**

   Use volume formula: $Volume = l \times w \times h$

   Then: $Volume = 8 \times 6 \times 10 = 480\ m^3$

   Use surface area formula: $Surface\ area = 2 \times (wh + lw + lh)$

   Then: $Surface\ area = 2 \times \big((6 \times 10) + (8 \times 6) + (8 \times 10)\big)$

   $= 2 \times (60 + 48 + 80) = 2 \times (188) = 376\ m^2$

2) Find the volume and surface area of this rectangular prism.

   **Solution:**

   Use volume formula: $Volume = l \times w \times h$

   Then: $Volume = 10 \times 8 \times 12 = 960\ m^3$

   Use surface area formula: $Surface\ area = 2 \times (wh + lw + lh)$

   Then: $Surface\ area = 2 \times \big((8 \times 12) + (10 \times 8) + (10 \times 12)\big)$

   $= 2 \times (96 + 80 + 120) = 2 \times (296) = 592\ m^2$

# Chapter 11: Practices

✍️ **Find the missing side?**

1)

2)

3)

4)

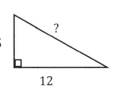

✍️ **Find the measure of the unknown angle in each figure.**

5)

6)

7)

8)

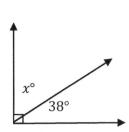

✍️ **In the following diagrams, solve for** x.

9)  $x =$

10)  $x = 9$

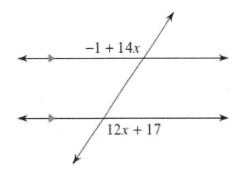

### ✎ Find the area of each triangle.

11)

12)

13)

14)

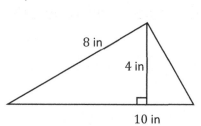

### ✎ Find the value of x and y in each triangle.

15)  $x = \underline{3\sqrt{3}}$  $y = \underline{6\sqrt{3}}$

16)  $x = \underline{\quad}$  $y = \underline{\quad}$

### ✎ Find the perimeter of each shape.

17)

18)

19)

20)

### ✎ Find the area of each trapezoid.

21)

22)

23)

24)

**ALEKS Mathematics Prep 2020-2021**

**Find the volume of each cube.**

25)

5 cm

125

26)

8 ft

27)
2 in

28)

6 miles

 **Find the volume of each Rectangular Prism.**

29)

8 cm

5 cm

3 cm

30)

12 m

9 m

6 m

31)

11 in

7 in

4 in

 **Find the volume of each Cylinder. Round your answer to the nearest tenth.** (π = 3.14)

32)

4 cm

14 cm

33)

6 m

8 m

34)

8 cm

10 cm

# Answers – Chapter 11

1) 4
2) 15
3) 12
4) 13
5) 60°
6) 80°
7) 90°
8) 52°
9) 4
10) 9
11) 24 *square unites*
12) 30 *square unites*
13) 64 $cm^2$
14) 20 $in^2$
15) $x = 3\sqrt{3}$ $y = 6\sqrt{3}$
16) $x = 8\sqrt{2}$   $y = 8$
17) 64 $cm$
18) 30 $ft$
19) 40 $in$
20) 30 $m$
21) 72 $m^2$
22) 108 $cm^2$
23) 60 $ft^2$
24) 21 $cm^2$
25) 125 $cm^3$
26) 512 $ft^3$
27) 8 $in^3$
28) 216 $miles^3$
29) 120 $cm^3$
30) 648 $m^3$ 308 $in^3$
31) 703.36 $cm^3$
32) 904.32 $m^3$
33) 2,009.6 $cm^3$

# Chapter 12:

# Statistics

**Math topics that you'll learn in this chapter:**

- ✓ Mean, Median, Mode, and Range of the Given Data

- ✓ Pie Graph

- ✓ Probability Problems

- ✓ Permutations and Combinations

# Mean, Median, Mode, and Range of the Given Data

☑ Mean: $\dfrac{sum\ of\ the\ data}{total\ number\ of\ data\ entires}$

☑ Mode: the value in the list that appears most often

☑ Median: is the middle number of a group of numbers arranged in order

by size.

☑ Range: the difference of the largest value and smallest value in the list

## Examples:

**1) What is the mode of these numbers?** $4, 5, 7, 5, 7, 4, 0, 4$

**Solution:** Mode: the value in the list that appears most often.
Therefore, the mode is number 4. There are three number 4 in the data.

**2) What is the median of these numbers?** $5, 10, 14, 9, 16, 19, 6$

**Solution:** Write the numbers in order: $5, 6, 9, 10, 14, 16, 19$

The median is the number in the middle. Therefore, the median is 10.

**3) What is the mean of these numbers?** $8, 2, 8, 5, 3, 2, 4, 8$

**Solution:** Mean: $\dfrac{sum\ of\ the\ data}{total\ number\ of\ data\ entires} = \dfrac{8+2+8+5+3+2+4+8}{8} = 5$

**4) What is the range in this list?** $4, 9, 13, 8, 15, 18, 5$

**Solution:** Range is the difference of the largest value and smallest value in the list. The largest value is 18 and the smallest value is 4. Then: $18 - 4 = 14$

# Pie Graph

☑ A Pie Chart is a circle chart divided into sectors, each sector represents the relative size of each value.

☑ Pie charts represent a snapshot of how a group is broken down into smaller pieces.

## Example:

A library has 820 books that include Mathematics, Physics, Chemistry, English and History. Use the following graph to answer the questions.

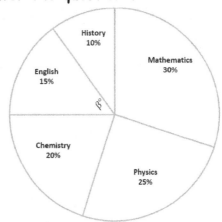

**1) What is the number of Mathematics books?**

**Solution:** Number of total books $= 820$

Percent of Mathematics books $= 30\% = 0.30$

Then, the number of Mathematics books:

$$0.30 \times 820 = 246$$

**2) What is the number of History books?**

**Solution:** Number of total books $= 820$

Percent of History books $= 10\% = 0.10$

Then: $0.10 \times 820 = 82$

**3) What is the number of Chemistry books?**

**Solution:** Number of total books $= 820$

Percent of Chemistry books $= 20\% = 0.20$

Then: $0.20 \times 820 = 164$

# Probability Problems

- ☑ Probability is the likelihood of something happening in the future. It is expressed as a number between zero (can never happen) to 1 (will always happen).

- ☑ Probability can be expressed as a fraction, a decimal, or a percent.

- ☑ Probability formula: $Probability = \frac{number\ of\ desired\ outcomes}{number\ of\ total\ outcomes}$

## Examples:

1) Anita's trick-or-treat bag contains 12 pieces of chocolate, 18 suckers, 18 pieces of gum, 24 pieces of licorice. If she randomly pulls a piece of candy from her bag, what is the probability of her pulling out a piece of sucker?

   **Solution:** $Probability = \frac{number\ of\ desired\ outcomes}{number\ of\ total\ outcomes}$

   Probability of pulling out a piece of sucker $= \frac{18}{12 + 18 + 18 + 24} = \frac{18}{72} = \frac{1}{4}$

2) A bag contains 20 balls: four green, five black, eight blue, a brown, a red and one white. If 19 balls are removed from the bag at random, what is the probability that a brown ball has been removed?

   **Solution:** If 19 balls are removed from the bag at random, there will be one ball in the bag. The probability of choosing a brown ball is 1 out of 20. Therefore, the probability of not choosing a brown ball is 19 out of 20 and the probability of having not a brown ball after removing 19 balls is the same.

# Permutations and Combinations

☑ Factorials are products, indicated by an exclamation mark. For example, $4! = 4 \times 3 \times 2 \times 1$(Remember that $0!$ is defined to be equal to 1.)

☑ Permutations: The number of ways to choose a sample of $k$ elements from a set of $n$ distinct objects where order does matter, and replacements are not allowed. For a permutation problem, use this formula:

$$_nP_k = \frac{n!}{(n-k)!}$$

☑ Combination: The number of ways to choose a sample of r elements from a set of n distinct objects where order does not matter, and replacements are not allowed. For a combination problem, use this formula:

$$_nC_r = \frac{n!}{r!\,(n-r)!}$$

## Examples:

1) *How many ways can the first and second place be awarded to 8 people?*

   **Solution:** Since the order matters, (the first and second place are different!) we need to use permutation formula where n is 8 and k is 2. Then: $\frac{n!}{(n-k)!} = \frac{8!}{(8-2)!} = \frac{8!}{6!} = \frac{8 \times 7 \times 6!}{6!}$, remove 6! from both sides of the fraction. Then: $\frac{8 \times 7 \times 6!}{6!} = 8 \times 7 = 56$

2) *How many ways can we pick a team of 2 people from a group of 6?*

   **Solution:** Since the order doesn't matter, we need to use a combination formula where n is 6 and r is 2. Then:$\frac{n!}{r!\,(n-r)!} = \frac{6!}{2!\,(6-2)!} = \frac{6!}{2!\,(4)!} = \frac{6 \times 5 \times 4!}{2!\,(4)!} = \frac{6 \times 5}{2 \times 1} = \frac{30}{2} = 15$

# Chapter 12: Practices

✍ *Find the values of the Given Data.*

1) 6, 12, 1, 1, 5

   Mode: __1__    Range: __11__

   Mean: __5__    Median: __5__

2) 5, 8, 3, 7, 4, 3

   Mode: ____    Range: ____

   Mean: ____    Median: ____

✍ The circle graph below shows all Jason's expenses for last month. Jason spent $864 on his bills last month.

3) How much did Jason spend on his car last month? _____

4) How much did Jason spend for foods last month? ____448____

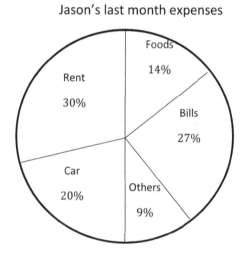

Jason's last month expenses

Foods 14%

Rent 30%

Bills 27%

Car 20%

Others 9%

✎ *Solve.*

5) Bag A contains 8 red marbles and 6 green marbles. Bag B contains 5 black marbles and 10 orange marbles. What is the probability of selecting a green marble at random from bag A? What is the probability of selecting a black marble at random from Bag B? _____          _____


✎ *Solve.*

6) Susan is baking cookies. She uses sugar, flour, butter, and eggs. How many different orders of ingredients can she try? _____

7) Jason is planning for his vacation. He wants to go to the museum, watch a movie, go to the beach, and play volleyball. How many different ways of ordering are there for him? ____24_____

8) In how many ways can a team of 10 basketball players choose a captain and co-captain? _____

9) How many ways can you give 3 balls to your 8 friends? _____

10) A professor will arrange her 8 students in a straight line. In how many ways can she do this? _____

# Answers – Chapter 12

1) Mode: 1 , Range: 11, Mean: 5, Median: 5

2) Mode: 3 , Range: 5 , Mean: 5, Median: 4.5

3) $640

4) $448

5) $\frac{3}{7}, \frac{1}{3}$

6) 24

7) 24

8) 90

9) 56

10) 40,320

# Chapter 13:

# Functions Operations

**Math topics that you'll learn in this chapter:**

- ✓ Function Notation Evaluation

- ✓ Adding and Subtracting Functions

- ✓ Multiplying and Dividing Functions

- ✓ Composition of Functions

# Function Notation and Evaluation

- ☑ Functions are mathematical operations that assign unique outputs to given inputs.
- ☑ Function notation is the way a function is written. It is meant to be a precise way of giving information about the function without a rather lengthy written explanation.
- ☑ The most popular function notation is $f(x)$ which is read "$f$ of $x$". Any letter can name a function. for example: $g(x)$, $h(x)$, etc.
- ☑ To evaluate a function, plug in the input (the given value or expression) for the function's variable (place holder, $x$).

## Examples:

1) Evaluate: $h(n) = n - 2$, find $h(4)$

   **Solution:** Substitute $n$ with 4: Then: $h(n) = n - 2 \rightarrow h(4) = 4 - 2 \rightarrow h(4) = 2$

2) Evaluate: $w(x) = 5x - 1$, find $w(3)$.

   **Solution:** Substitute $x$ with 3: Then: $w(x) = 5x - 1 \rightarrow w(3) = 5(3) - 1 = 15 - 1 = 14$

3) Evaluate: $f(x) = x^2 - 2$, find $h(2)$.

   **Solution:** Substitute $x$ with 2: Then: $f(x) = x^2 - 2 \rightarrow f(2) = (2)^2 - 2 = 4 - 2 = 2$

4) Evaluate: $p(x) = 2x^2 - 4$, find $p(3a)$.

   **Solution:** Substitute $x$ with $3a$: Then: $p(x) = 2x^2 - 4 \rightarrow p(3a) = 2(3a)^2 - 4 \rightarrow$

   $$p(3a) = 2(9a^2) - 4 = 18a^2 - 4$$

# Adding and Subtracting Functions

☑ Just like we can add and subtract numbers and expressions, we can add or subtract two functions and simplify or evaluate them. The result is a new function.

☑ For two functions $f(x)$ and $g(x)$, we can create two new functions:
$(f + g)(x) = f(x) + g(x)$ and $(f - g)(x) = f(x) - g(x)$

## Examples:

**1)** $g(x) = a - 1, f(a) = a + 2,$ **Find:** $(g + f)(a)$

    **Solution:** $(g + f)(a) = g(a) + f(a)$

    Then: $(g + f)(a) = (a - 1) + (a + 2) = 2a + 1$

**2)** $f(x) = 2x - 2, g(x) = x - 4,$ **Find:** $(f - g)(x)$

    **Solution:** $(f - g)(x) = f(x) - g(x)$

    Then: $(f - g)(x) = (2x - 2) - (x - 4) = 2x - 2 - x + 4 = x + 2$

**3)** $g(x) = x^2 - 4, f(x) = 2x + 3,$ **Find:** $(g + f)(x)$

    **Solution:** $(g + f)(x) = g(x) + f(x)$

    Then: $(g + f)(x) = (x^2 - 4) + (2x + 3) = x^2 + 2x - 1$

**4)** $f(x) = 2x^2 + 5, g(x) = 3x - 1,$ **Find:** $(f - g)(5)$

    **Solution:** $(f - g)(x) = f(x) - g(x)$

    Then: $(f - g)(x) = (2x^2 + 5) - (3x - 1) = 2x^2 + 5 - 3x + 1 = 2x^2 - 3x + 6$

    Substitute $x$ with 5: $(g - f)(5) = 2(5)^2 - 3(5) + 6 = 50 - 15 + 6 = 41$

# Multiplying and Dividing Functions

☑ Just like we can multiply and divide numbers and expressions, we can multiply and divide two functions and simplify or evaluate them.

☑ For two functions $f(x)$ and $g(x)$, we can create two new functions:

$$(f.g)(x) = f(x).g(x) \text{ and } \left(\frac{f}{g}\right)(x) = \frac{f(x)}{g(x)}$$

## Examples:

1) $g(x) = x - 2, f(x) = x + 3$, Find: $(g.f)(x)$

   **Solution:** $(g.f)(x) = g(x).f(x) = (x - 2)(x + 3) = x^2 + 3x - 2x - 6$

2) $f(x) = x + 4, h(x) = x - 6$, Find: $\left(\frac{f}{h}\right)(x)$

   **Solution:** $\left(\frac{f}{h}\right)(x) = \frac{f(x)}{h(x)} = \frac{x+4}{x-6}$

3) $g(x) = x + 5, f(x) = x - 2$, Find: $(g.f)(4)$

   **Solution:** $(g.f)(x) = g(x).f(x) = (x + 5)(x - 2) = x^2 - 2x + 5x - 10 = x^2 + 3x - 10$

   Substitute $x$ with 4: $(g.f)(x) = (4)^2 + 3(4) - 10 = 16 + 12 - 10 = 18$

4) $f(x) = 2x + 3, h(x) = x + 8$, Find: $\left(\frac{f}{h}\right)(-1)$

   **Solution:** $\left(\frac{f}{h}\right)(x) = \frac{f(x)}{h(x)} = \frac{2x+3}{x+8}$

   Substitute $x$ with $-1$: $\left(\frac{f}{h}\right)(x) = \frac{2x+3}{x+8} = \frac{2(-1)+3}{(-1)+8} = \frac{1}{7}$

# Composition of Functions

☑ "Composition of functions" simply means combining two or more functions in a way where the output from one function becomes the input for the next function.

☑ The notation used for composition is: $(fog)(x) = f(g(x))$ and is read "$f$ composed with $g$ of $x$" or "$f$ of $g$ of $x$".

## Examples:

1) **Using** f(x) = x − 5 **and** g(x) = 2x, **find** (fog)(x).

   **Solution:** $(fog)(x) = f\big(g(x)\big)$. Then: $(fog)(x) = f\big(g(x)\big) = f(2x)$

   Now find $f(2x)$ by substituting $x$ with $2x$ in $f(x)$ function. Then: f(x) = x − 5

   $(x \to 2x) \to f(2x) = (2x) - 5 = 2x - 5$

2) **Using** f(x) = x + 6, **and** g(x) = x − 2, **find** (gof)(x).

   **Solution:** $(f \ o \ g)(x) = f(g(x))$. Then: $(g \ o \ f)(x) = g\big(f(x)\big) = g(x + 6)$, now substitute $x$ in $g(x)$ by $(x + 6)$. Then: $g(x + 6) = (x + 6) - 2 = x + 6 - 2 = x + 4$

   Substitute $x$ with −1: $(g \ o \ f)(-1) = g\big(f(x)\big) = x + 4 = -1 + 4 = 3$

3) **Using** f(x) = 2x − 2 **and** g(x) = 2x, **find:** $f(g(5))$

   **Solution:** First, find $g(5)$): $g(x) = 2x \to$ g(5) = 2(5) = 10

   Then: $f\big(g(5)\big) = f(10)$. Now, find $f(10)$ by substituting $x$ with 10 in $f(x)$ function.

   Then: $f\big(g(5)\big) = f(10) = 2(10) - 2 = 20 - 2 = 18$

# Function Inverses

☑ An inverse function is a function that reverses another function:

if the function $f$ applied to an input $x$ gives a result of $y$, then

applying its inverse function $g$ to $y$ gives the result $x$.

$f(x) = y$ if and only if $g(y) = x$

☑ The inverse function of $f(x)$ is usually shown by $f^{-1}(x)$.

## Examples:

**1) Find the inverse of the function:** $f(x) = 2x - 1$

*Solution:* First, replace $f(x)$ with y: $y = 2x - 1$, Then, replace all $x$'s with y and all y's with

$x$: $x = 2y - 1$, Now, solve for y: $x = 2x - 1 \rightarrow x + 1 = 2y \rightarrow \frac{1}{2}x + \frac{1}{2} = y$

Finally replace y with $f^{-1}(x)$: $f^{-1}(x) = \frac{1}{2}x + \frac{1}{2}$

**2) Find the inverse of the function:** $g^{-1}(x) = \frac{1}{5}x + 3$

*Solution:* $g(x) = \frac{1}{5}x + 3 \rightarrow y = \frac{1}{5}x + 3 \rightarrow$ replace all $x$'s with y and all y's with x

$x = \frac{1}{5}y + 3$, solve for y: $\rightarrow x - 3 = \frac{1}{5}y \rightarrow 5(x - 3) = y \rightarrow g^{-1}(x) = 5x - 15$

**3) Find the inverse of the function:** $h(x) = \sqrt{x} + 6$

*Solution:* $h(x) = \sqrt{x} + 6 \rightarrow y = \sqrt{x} + 6$, replace all x's with y and all y's with x

$\rightarrow x = \sqrt{y} + 6 \rightarrow x - 6 = \sqrt{y} \rightarrow (x - 6)^2 = (\sqrt{y})^2 \rightarrow x^2 - 12x + 36 = y$

$\rightarrow h^{-1}(x) = x^2 - 12x + 36$

# Chapter 13: Practices

✎ **Evaluate each function.**

1) $g(n) = 6n - 3$, find $g(-2)$

$-15$

2) $h(x) = -8x + 12$, find $h(3)$

_____

3) $k(n) = 14 - 3n$, find $k(3)$

_____

4) $g(x) = 4x - 4$, find $g(-2)$

_____

5) $k(n) = 8n - 7$, find $k(4)$

_____

6) $w(n) = -2n + 14$, find $w(5)$

_____

✎ **Perform the indicated operation.**

7) $f(x) = x + 6$

$g(x) = 3x + 3$

Find $(f - g)(2)$

_____

8) $g(x) = x - 3$

$f(x) = -x - 4$

Find $(g - f)(-2)$

_____

9) $h(t) = 5t + 4$

$g(t) = 2t + 2$

Find $(h + g)(-1)$

_____

10) $g(a) = 3a - 5$

$f(a) = a^2 + 6$

Find $(g + f)(3)$

$19$

11) $g(x) = 4x - 5$

$h(x) = 6x^2 + 5$

Find $(g - f)(-2)$

_____

12) $h(x) = x^2 + 3$

$g(x) = -4x + 1$

Find $(h + g)(4)$

$4$

*📝 Perform the indicated operation.*

13) $g(x) = x + 2$    6

    $f(x) = x + 3$    7

    Find $(g.f)(4)$

    ___42___

14) $f(x) = 2x$

    $h(x) = -x + 6$

    Find $(f.h)(-2)$

    _____

15) $g(a) = a + 2$

    $h(a) = 2a - 3$

    Find $(g.h)(5)$

    _____

16) $f(x) = 2x + 4$

    $h(x) = 4x - 2$

    Find $\left(\frac{f}{h}\right)(2)$

    _____

17) $f(x) = a^2 - 2$

    $g(x) = -4 + 3a$

    Find $\left(\frac{f}{g}\right)(2)$

    _____

18) $g(a) = 4a + 6$

    $f(a) = 2a - 8$

    Find $\left(\frac{g}{f}\right)(3)$

    _____

*📝 Using $f(x) = 2x + 5$ and $g(x) = x - 2$, find:*

19) $g(f(2)) = $ ___7___

20) $g(f(-2)) = $ _____

21) $f(g(5)) = $ _____

22) $f(f(4)) = $ _____

23) $g(f(3)) = $ _____

24) $g(f(-3)) = $ _____

*📝 Find the inverse of each function.*

25)   $f(x) = \frac{1}{x} - 6 \rightarrow f^{-1}(x) = $   1

26)   $g(x) = \frac{7}{-x-3} \rightarrow g^{-1}(x) = $   $x + 6$

27)   $h(x) = \frac{x+9}{3} \rightarrow h^{-1}(x) = $

28)   $h(x) = \frac{2x-10}{4} \rightarrow h^{-1}(x) = $

# Answers – Chapter 13

1) $-15$

2) $-12$

3) $5$

4) $-12$

5) $25$

6) $4$

7) $-1$

8) $-3$

9) $-1$

10) $19$

11) $-42$

12) $4$

13) $42$

14) $-32$

15) $49$

16) $\frac{4}{3}$

17) $1$

18) $-9$

19) $7$

20) $-1$

21) $11$

22) $31$

23) $9$

24) $-3$

25) $\frac{1}{x+6}$

26) $-\frac{7=3x}{x}$

27) $3x - 9$

28) $2x + 5$

# Chapter 14:

# Quadratic

**Math topics that you'll learn in this Chapter:**

✓ Solving a Quadratic Equation

✓ Graphing Quadratic Functions

✓ Solving Quadratic Inequalities

✓ Graphing Quadratic Inequalities

# Solving a Quadratic Equations

☑ Write the equation in the form of: $ax^2 + bx + c = 0$

☑ Factorize the quadratic, set each factor equal to zero and solve.

☑ Use quadratic formula if you couldn't factorize the quadratic.

☑ Quadratic formula: $x = \dfrac{-b \pm \sqrt{b^2 - 4ac}}{2a}$

## Examples:

Find the solutions of each quadratic.

1) $x^2 + 7x + 12 = 0$

**Solution:** Factor the quadratic by grouping. We need to find two numbers whose sum is 7 (from $7x$) and whose product is 12. Those numbers are 3 and 4. Then: $x^2 + 7x + 12 = 0 \rightarrow$ $x^2 + 3x + 4x + 12 = 0 \rightarrow (x^2 + 3x) + (4x + 12) = 0$, Now, find common factors: $(x^2 + 3x) = x(x + 3)$ and $(4x + 12) = 3(x + 4)$. We have two expressions $((x^2 + 3x)$ and $(4x + 12))$ and their common factor is $(x + 3)$. Then: $(x^2 + 3x) + (4x + 12) = 0 \rightarrow$ $x(x + 3) + 4(x + 3) = 0 \rightarrow (x + 3)(x + 4) = 0$. The product of two expressions is 0. Then:

$(x + 3) = 0 \rightarrow x = -3$ or $(x + 4) = 0 \rightarrow x = -4$

2) $x^2 + 5x + 6 = 0$

**Solution:** Use quadratic formula: $x_{1,2} = \dfrac{-b \pm \sqrt{b^2 - 4ac}}{2a}$, $a = 1, b = 5$ and $c = 6$

Then: $= \dfrac{-5 \pm \sqrt{5^2 - 4 \times 1(6)}}{2(1)}$, $x_1 = \dfrac{-5 + \sqrt{5^2 - 4 \times 1(6)}}{2(1)} = -2$, $x_2 = \dfrac{-5 - \sqrt{5^2 - 4 \times 1(6)}}{2(1)} = -3$

3) $x^2 + 6x + 8 = 0$

**Solution:** Factor: $x^2 + 6x + 8 = 0 \rightarrow (x + 2)(x + 4) = 0 \rightarrow x = -2, or\ x = -4$

# Graphing Quadratic Functions

✓ Quadratic functions in vertex form: $y = a(x - h)^2 + k$ where $(h, k)$ is the vertex of the function. The axis of symmetry is $x = h$

✓ Quadratic functions in standard form: $y = ax^2 + bx + c$ where $x = -\frac{b}{2a}$ is the value of $x$ in the vertex of the function.

✓ To graph a quadratic function, first find the vertex, then substitute some values for $x$ and solve for $y$. (Remember that the graph of a quadratic function is a U-shaped curve and it is called "parabola".)

## Examples:

**Sketch the graph of $y = (x + 2)^2 - 3$.**

**Solution:**

Quadratic functions in vertex form: $y = a(x - h)^2 + k$ and $(h, k)$ is the vertex. Then, the vertex of $y = (x + 2)^2 - 3$ is $(-2, -3)$.

Substitute zero for $x$ and solve for $y$:

$y = (0 + 2)^2 - 3 = 1$.

The $y$ Intercept is $(0, 1)$.

Now, you can simply graph the quadratic function. Notice that quadratic function is a U-shaped curve.

ALEKS Mathematics Prep 2020-2021

# Solving Quadratic Inequalities

☑ A quadratic inequality is one that can be written in the standard form of $ax^2 + bx + c > 0$ (or substitute $<, \leq,$ or $\geq$ for $>$).

☑ Solving a quadratic inequality is like solving equations. We need to find the solutions (the zeroes).

☑ To solve quadratic inequalities, first find quadratic equations. Then choose a test value between zeroes. Finally, find interval(s), such as $> 0$ or $< 0$.

## Examples:

1) **Solve quadratic inequality.** $x^2 + x - 6 > 0$

**Solution:** First solve $x^2 + x - 6 = 0$ by factoring. Then: $x^2 + x - 6 = 0 \rightarrow$ $(x - 2)(x + 3) = 0$. The product of two expressions is 0. Then: $(x - 2) = 0 \rightarrow x = 2$ or $(x + 3) = 0 \rightarrow x = -3$. Now, choose a value between 2 and $-3$. Let's choose 0. Then:

$$x = 0 \rightarrow x^2 + x - 6 > 0 \rightarrow (0)^2 + (0) - 6 > 0 \rightarrow -6 > 0$$

$-6$ is not greater than 0. Therefore, all values between 2 and $-3$ are NOT the solution of this quadratic inequality. The solution is: $x > 2$ and $x < -3$. To represent the solution, we can use interval notation, in which solution sets are indicated with parentheses or brackets. The solutions $x > 2$ and $x < -3$ represented as: $(\infty, -3) \cup (2, \infty)$

Solution $x \geq 2$ represented as: $[2, \infty)$

2) **Solve quadratic inequality.** $x^2 - 2x - 8 \geq 0$

**Solution:** First solve: $x^2 - 2x - 8 = 0$, Factor: $x^2 - 2x - 8 = 0 \rightarrow (x - 4)(x + 2) = 0$.

$-2$ and 4 are the solutions. Choose a point between $-2$ and 4. Let's choose 0. Then:

$x = 0 \rightarrow x^2 - 2x - 8 \geq 0 \rightarrow (0)^2 - 2(0) - 8 \geq 0 \rightarrow -8 \geq 0$. This is NOT true. So, the solution is: $x \leq -2$ or $x \geq 4$ (using interval notation the solution is: $(\infty, -2] \cup [4, \infty)$

# Graphing Quadratic Inequalities

✓ A quadratic inequality is in the form $y > ax^2 + bx + c$ (or substitute $<, \leq,$ or $\geq$ for $>$).

✓ To graph a quadratic inequality, start by graphing the quadratic parabola. Then fill in the region either inside or outside of it, depending on the inequality.

✓ Choose a testing point and check the solution section.

## Example:

**Sketch the graph of $y > 2x^2$**

**Solution:**

First, graph the quadratic $y = 2x^2$

Since, the inequality sing is $>$, we need to use dash lines.

Now, choose a testing point inside the parabola. Let's choose (0,2).

$y > 2x^2 \rightarrow 2 > 2(0)^2 \rightarrow 2 > 0$

This is true. So, inside the parabola is the solution section.

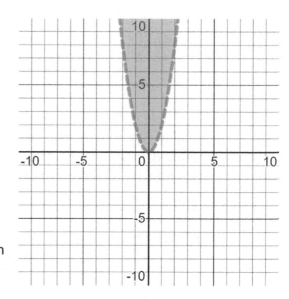

# Chapter 14: Practices

✍ **Solve each equation by factoring or using the quadratic formula.**

1) $x^2 - 4x - 32 = 0$

$\underline{\phantom{8,-4}} 8, -4 \qquad \dfrac{4 \pm \sqrt{4(1)(-32)}}{2}$

2) $x^2 - 2x - 63 = 0$

_____

3) $x^2 + 17x + 72 = 0$

_____

4) $x^2 + 14x + 48 = 0$

_____

5) $x^2 + 5x - 24 = 0$

_____

6) $x^2 + 15x + 36 = 0$

_____

✍ **Sketch the graph of each function.**

7) $y = (x + 1)^2 - 2$

8) $y = (x - 1)^2 + 3$

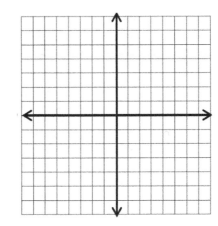

✍ *Solve each quadratic inequality.*

9) $x^2 - 4 < 0$

____

10) $x^2 - 9 > 0$

____

11) $x^2 - 5x - 6 < 0$

$-1 < x < 6$

12) $x^2 + 8x - 20 > 0$

____

13) $x^2 + 10x - 24 \geq 0$

____

14) $x^2 + 17x + 72 \leq 0$

$-9 \leq x \leq 8$

✍ *Sketch the graph of each quadratic inequality.*

15) $y < -2x^2$

16) $y > 3x^2$

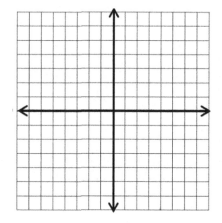

# Answers – Chapter 14

1) $x^2 - 4x - 32 = 0$

$x = 8, x = -4$

2) $x^2 - 2x - 63 = 0$

$x = 9, x = -7$

3) $x^2 + 17x + 72 = 0$

$x = -9, x = -8$

4) $x^2 + 14x + 48 = 0$

$x = -6, x = -8$

5) $x^2 + 5x - 24 = 0$

$x = 3, x = -8$

6) $x^2 + 15x + 36 = 0$

$x = -12, x = -3$

7) $y = (x + 1)^2 - 2$

8) $y = (x - 1)^2 + 3$

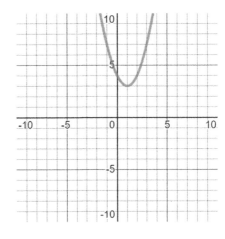

9) $x^2 - 4 < 0$

$-2 < x < 2$

10) $x^2 - 9 > 0$

$-3 < x < 3$

11) $x^2 - 5x - 6 < 0$

$-1 < x < 6$

12) $x^2 + 8x - 20 > 0$

$x < -10 \ or \ x > 2$

13) $x^2 + 10x - 24 \geq 0$

$x \leq -12 \ or \ x \geq 2$

14) $x^2 + 17x + 72 \leq 0$

$-9 \leq x \leq -8$

15) $y < -2x^2$

16) $y > 3x^2$

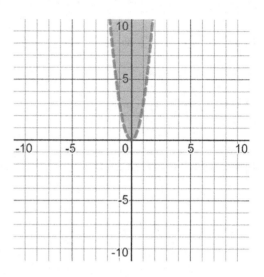

136

# Chapter 15:

# Complex Numbers

**Math topics that you'll learn in this chapter:**

- ✓ Adding and Subtracting Complex Numbers

- ✓ Multiplying and Dividing Complex Number

- ✓ Rationalizing Imaginary Denominators

# Adding and Subtracting Complex Numbers

☑ A complex number is expressed in the form $a + bi$, where $a$ and $b$ are real numbers, and $i$, which is called an imaginary number, is a solution of the equation $x^2 = -1$

☑ For adding complex numbers:

$$(a + bi) + (c + di) = (a + c) + (b + d)i$$

☑ For subtracting complex numbers:

$$(a + bi) - (c + di) = (a - c) + (b - d)i$$

## Examples:

1) Solve: $(8 + 4i) + (6 - 2i)$

   **Solution:** Remove parentheses: $(8 + 4i) + (6 - 2i) = 8 + 4i + 6 - 2i$

   Combine like terms: $(8 + 6) + (4i - 2i) = 14 + 2i$

2) Solve: $(10 + 8i) + (8 - 3i)$

   **Solution:** Remove parentheses: $(10 + 8i) + (8 - 3i) = 10 + 8i + 8 - 3i$

   Group like terms: $(10 + 8) + (8i - 3i) = 18 + 5i$

3) Solve: $(-5 - 3i) - (2 + 4i)$

   **Solution:** Remove parentheses by multiplying $-1$ to the second parentheses:

   $$(-5 - 3i) - (2 + 4i) = -5 - 3i - 2 - 4i$$

   Combine like terms: $(-5 - 2) + (-3i - 4i) = -7 - 7i$

**ALEKS Mathematics Prep 2020-2021**

# Multiplying and Dividing Complex Numbers

☑ You can use FOIL (first-out-in-last) method or the following rule to multiply imaginary numbers. Remember that: $i^2 = -1$

$$(a + bi) + (c + di) = (ac - bd) + (ad + bc)i$$

☑ To divide complex numbers, you need to find the conjugate of the denominator. Conjugate of $(a + bi)$ is $(a - bi)$.

☑ Dividing complex numbers: $\frac{a+bi}{c+di} = \frac{a+bi}{c+di} \times \frac{c-di}{c-di} = \frac{ac+bd}{c^2+d^2} + \frac{bc-ad}{c^2+d^2}i$

## Examples:

1) Solve: $\frac{6-2i}{2+i}$

**Solution:** The conjugate of $(2 + i)$ is $(2 - i)$. Use the rule for dividing complex numbers:

$$\frac{a+bi}{c+di} = \frac{a+bi}{c+di} \times \frac{c-di}{c-di} = \frac{ac+bd}{c^2+d^2} + \frac{bc-ad}{c^2+d^2}i \rightarrow$$

$$\frac{6-2i}{2+i} \times \frac{2-i}{2-i} = \frac{6 \times (2) + (-2)(1)}{2^2 + (1)^2} + \frac{-2 \times 2 - (6)(1)}{2^2 + (1)^2}i = \frac{10}{5} + \frac{-10}{5}i = 2 - 2i$$

2) Solve: $(2 - 3i)(6 - 3i)$

**Solution:** Use the multiplication of imaginary numbers rule:

$$(a + bi) + (c + di) = (ac - bd) + (ad + bc)i$$

$$(2 \times 6 - (-3)(-3)) + (2(-3) + (-3) \times 6)i = 3 - 24i$$

3) Solve: $\frac{3-2i}{4+i}$

**Solution:** Use the rule for dividing complex numbers: $\frac{a+bi}{c+di} = \frac{a+bi}{c+di} \times \frac{c-di}{c-di} =$

$\frac{ac+bd}{c^2+d^2} + \frac{bc-ad}{c^2+d^2}i \rightarrow \frac{3-2i}{4+i} \times \frac{4-i}{4-i} = \frac{(3 \times 4 + (-2) \times 1) + (-2 \times 4 - 3 \times 1)i}{4^2 + 1^2} = \frac{10-11i}{17} = \frac{10}{17} - \frac{11}{17}i$

# Rationalizing Imaginary Denominators

☑ Step 1: Find the conjugate (it's the denominator with different sign between the two terms).

☑ Step 2: Multiply numerator and denominator by the conjugate.

☑ Step 3: Simplify if needed.

## Examples:

1) Solve: $\dfrac{4-3i}{6i}$

**Solution:** Multiply both numerator and denominator by $\dfrac{i}{i}$ :

$$\frac{4-3i}{6i} = \frac{(4-3i)(i)}{6i(i)} = \frac{(4)(i)-(3i)(i)}{6(i^2)} = \frac{4i-3i^2}{6(-1)} = \frac{4i-3(-1)}{-6} = \frac{4i}{-6} + \frac{3}{-6} = -\frac{1}{2} - \frac{2}{3}i$$

2) Solve: $\dfrac{6i}{2-i}$

**Solution:**

Multiply both numerator and denominator by the conjugate $\dfrac{2+i}{2+i}$: $\dfrac{6i(2+i)}{(2-i)(2+i)} =$

Apply complex arithmetic rule: $(a+bi)(a-bi) = a^2 + b^2$

$2^2 + (-1)^2 = 5$, then: $\dfrac{6i(2+i)}{(2-i)(2+i)} = \dfrac{-6+12i}{5} = -\dfrac{6}{5} + \dfrac{12}{5}i$

3) Solve: $\dfrac{8-2i}{2i}$

**Solution:** Factor 2 from both sides: $\dfrac{8-2i}{2i} = \dfrac{2(4-i)}{2i}$, divide both sides by 2: $\dfrac{2(4-i)}{2i} = \dfrac{(4-i)}{i}$

Multiply both numerator and denominator by $\dfrac{i}{i}$: $\dfrac{(4-i)}{i} = \dfrac{(4-i)}{i} \times \dfrac{i}{i} = \dfrac{(4i-i^2)}{i^2} = \dfrac{1+4i}{-1} = -1 - 4i$

**ALEKS Mathematics Prep 2020-2021**

# Chapter 15: Practices

## ✍ Evaluate.

1) $(-5i) - (7i) =$ _-12i_

2) $(-2i) + (-8i) =$

3) $(2i) - (6 + 3i) =$

4) $(4 - 6i) + (-2i) =$

5) $(-7i) + (4 + 5i) =$

6) $10 + (-2 - 6i) =$

7) $(-3i) - (9 + 2i) =$

8) $(4 + 6i) - (-3i) =$ _4 + 9i_

## ✍ Calculate.

9) $(3 - 2i)(4 - 3i) =$ _6 - 17i_

10) $(6 + 2i)(3 + 2i) =$

11) $(8 - i)(4 - 2i) =$

12) $(2 - 4i)(3 - 5i) =$

13) $(5 + 6i)(3 + 2i) =$

14) $(5 + 3i)(9 + 2i) =$

## ✍ Simplify.

15) $\frac{3}{2i} =$

16) $\frac{8}{-3i} =$ _$\frac{8i}{3}$_

17) $\frac{-9}{2i} =$

18) $\frac{2 - 3i}{-5i} =$

19) $\frac{4 - 5i}{-2i} =$

20) $\frac{8 + 3i}{2i} =$ _$-\frac{3}{2} + 4i$_

# Answers – Chapter 15

1) $-12i$

2) $-10i$

3) $-6 - i$

4) $4 - 8i$

5) $4 - 2i$

6) $8 - 6i$

7) $-9 - 5i$

8) $4 + 9i$

9) $6 - 17i$

10) $14 + 18i$

11) $30 - 20i$

12) $-14 - 22i$

13) $3 + 28i$

14) $39 + 37i$

15) $-\dfrac{3i}{2}$

16) $\dfrac{8i}{3}$

17) $-\dfrac{9i}{2}$

18) $\dfrac{3}{5} + \dfrac{2}{5}i$

19) $\dfrac{5}{2} + 2i$

20) $-\dfrac{3}{2} + 4i$

# Chapter 16:

# Radicals

**Math topics that you'll learn in this chapter:**

✓ Simplifying Radical Expressions

✓ Adding and Subtracting Radical Expressions

✓ Multiplying Radical Expressions

✓ Rationalizing Denominators and Numerators of Radical Expressions

✓ Radical Equations

✓ Domain and Range of Radical Functions

# Simplifying Radical Expressions

☑ Find the prime factors of the numbers or expressions inside the radical.

☑ Use radical properties to simplify the radical expression:

$$\sqrt[n]{x^a} = x^{\frac{a}{n}}, \ \sqrt[n]{xy} = x^{\frac{1}{n}} \times y^{\frac{1}{n}}, \ \sqrt[n]{\frac{x}{y}} = \frac{x^{\frac{1}{n}}}{y^{\frac{1}{n}}}, \text{ and } \sqrt[n]{x} \times \sqrt[n]{y} = \sqrt[n]{xy}$$

## Examples:

**1) Find the square root of $\sqrt{144x^2}$.**

**Solution:** Find the factor of the expression $144x^2$: $144 = 12 \times 12$ and

$x^2 = x \times x$, now use radical rule: $\sqrt[n]{a^n} = a$, Then: $\sqrt{12^2} = 12$ and $\sqrt{x^2} = x$

Finally: $\sqrt{144x^2} = \sqrt{12^2} \times \sqrt{x^2} = 12 \times x = 12x$

**2) Write this radical in exponential form. $\sqrt[3]{x^4}$**

**Solution:** To write a radical in exponential form, use this rule: $\sqrt[n]{x^a} = x^{\frac{a}{n}}$

Then: $\sqrt[3]{x^4} = x^{\frac{4}{3}}$

**3) Simplify. $\sqrt{8x^3}$**

**Solution:** First factor the expression $8x^3$: $8x^3 = 2^3 \times x \times x \times x$, we need to find perfect

squares: $8x^3 = 2^2 \times 2 \times x^2 \times x = 2^2 \times x^2 \times 2x$, Then: $\sqrt{8x^3} = \sqrt{2^2 \times x^2} \times \sqrt{2x}$

Now use radical rule: $\sqrt[n]{a^n} = a$, Then: $\sqrt{2^2 \times x^2} \times \sqrt{(2x)} = 2x \times \sqrt{2x} = 2x\sqrt{2x}$

ALEKS Mathematics Prep 2020-2021

# Adding and Subtracting Radical Expressions

- ☑ Only numbers and expressions that have the same radical part can be added or subtracted.

- ☑ Remember, combining "unlike" radical terms is not possible.

- ☑ For numbers with the same radical part, just add or subtract factors outside the radicals.

## Examples:

*1) Simplify:* $6\sqrt{2} + 5\sqrt{2}$

**Solution:** Since we have the same radical parts, then we can add these two

radicals: Add like terms: $6\sqrt{2} + 5\sqrt{2} = 11\sqrt{2}$

*2) Simplify:* $2\sqrt{8} - 2\sqrt{2}$

**Solution:** The two radical parts are not the same. First, we need to simplify the

$2\sqrt{8}$. Then: $2\sqrt{8} = 2\sqrt{4 \times 2} = 2(\sqrt{4})(\sqrt{2}) = 4\sqrt{2}$

Now, combine like terms: $2\sqrt{8} - 2\sqrt{2} = 4\sqrt{2} - 2\sqrt{2} = 2\sqrt{2}$

# Multiplying Radical Expressions

To multiply radical expressions:

- ☑ Multiply the numbers and expressions outside of the radicals.

- ☑ Multiply the numbers and expressions inside the radicals.

- ☑ Simplify if needed.

## Examples:

**1) Evaluate.** $2\sqrt{5} \times \sqrt{3}$

**Solution:** Multiply the numbers outside of the radicals and the radical parts.

Then: $2\sqrt{5} \times \sqrt{3} = 2 \times 1 \times \sqrt{5} \times \sqrt{3} = 2\sqrt{15}$

**2) Simplify.** $3x\sqrt{3} \times 4\sqrt{x}$

**Solution:** Multiply the numbers outside of the radicals and the radical parts.

Then, simplify: $3x\sqrt{3} \times 4\sqrt{x} = (3x \times 4) \times (\sqrt{3} \times \sqrt{x}) = (12x)(\sqrt{3x}) = 12x\sqrt{3x}$

# Rationalizing of Radical Expressions

☑ Radical expressions cannot be in the denominator. (number in the bottom)

☑ To get rid of the radical in the denominator, multiply both numerator and denominator by the radical in the denominator.

☑ If there is a radical and another integer in the denominator, multiply both numerator and denominator by the conjugate of the denominator.

☑ The conjugate of $(a + b)$ is $(a - b)$ and vice versa.

## Examples:

1) **Simplify** $\dfrac{5}{\sqrt{6} - 4}$

Multiply by the conjugate: $\dfrac{\sqrt{6} + 4}{\sqrt{6} + 4} \rightarrow \dfrac{5}{\sqrt{6} - 4} \times \dfrac{\sqrt{6} + 4}{\sqrt{6} + 4}$

$$\left(\sqrt{6} - 4\right)\left(\sqrt{6} + 4\right) = -10 \text{ then: } \dfrac{5}{\sqrt{6} - 4} \times \dfrac{\sqrt{6} + 4}{\sqrt{6} + 4} = \dfrac{5(\sqrt{6} + 4)}{-10}$$

Use the fraction rule: $\dfrac{a}{-b} = -\dfrac{a}{b} \rightarrow \dfrac{5(\sqrt{6} + 4)}{-10} = -\dfrac{5(\sqrt{6} + 4)}{10} = -\dfrac{1}{2}\left(\sqrt{6} + 4\right)$

2) **Simplify** $\dfrac{2}{\sqrt{3} - 1}$

Multiply by the conjugate: $\dfrac{\sqrt{3} + 1}{\sqrt{3} + 1}$

$$\dfrac{2}{\sqrt{3} - 1} \times \dfrac{\sqrt{3} + 1}{\sqrt{3} + 1} = \dfrac{2(\sqrt{3} + 1)}{2} \rightarrow = \left(\sqrt{3} + 1\right)$$

# Radical Equations

☑ Isolate the radical on one side of the equation.

☑ Square both sides of the equation to remove the radical.

☑ Solve the equation for the variable.

☑ Plugin the answer (answers) into the original equation to avoid extraneous values.

## Examples:

1) **Solve** $\sqrt{x} - 5 = 15$

**Solution:** Add 5 to both sides: $\sqrt{x} = 20$, Square both sides: $(\sqrt{x})^2 = 20^2 \rightarrow x = 400$

Plugin the value of 400 for $x$ in the original equation and check the answer:

$x = 400 \rightarrow \sqrt{x} - 5 = \sqrt{400} - 5 = 20 - 5 = 15$, So, the value of 400 for $x$ is correct.

2) **What is the value of $x$ in this equation?** $2\sqrt{x + 1} = 4$

**Solution:** Divide both sides by 2. Then: $2\sqrt{x + 1} = 4 \rightarrow \frac{2\sqrt{x+1}}{2} = \frac{4}{2} \rightarrow \sqrt{x + 1} = 2$

Square both sides: $\left(\sqrt{(x + 1)}\right)^2 = 2^2$, Then $x + 1 = 4 \rightarrow x = 3$

Substitute $x$ by 3 in the original equation and check the answer:

$$x = 15 \rightarrow 2\sqrt{x + 1} = 2\sqrt{3 + 1} = 2\sqrt{4} = 2(2) = 4$$

So, the value of 3 for $x$ is correct.

# Domain and Range of Radical Functions

☑ To find the domain of the function, find all possible values of the variable inside radical.

☑ Remember that having a negative number under the square root symbol is not possible. (For cubic roots, we can have negative numbers)

☑ To find the range, plugin the minimum and maximum values of the variable inside radical.

## Example:

**Find the domain and range of the radical function.** $y = \sqrt{x - 3}$

**Solution:** For domain: Find non-negative values for radicals: $x - 3 \geq 0$

Domain of functions: $\sqrt{f(x)} \rightarrow f(x) \geq 0$, Then solve $x - 3 \geq 0 \rightarrow x \geq 3$

Domain of the function $y = \sqrt{x - 3}$: $x \geq 3$

For range: The range of a radical function of the form $c\sqrt{ax + b} + k$ is:

$$f(x) \geq k$$

For the function $y = \sqrt{x - 3}$, the value of $k$ is $0$. Then: $f(x) \geq 0$

Range of the function $y = \sqrt{x - 3}$: $f(x) \geq 0$

# Chapter 16: Practices

✎ *Simplify.*

1) $\sqrt{256y} =$   $16\sqrt{y}$

2) $\sqrt{900} =$

3) $\sqrt{144a^2b} =$

4) $\sqrt{36 \times 9} =$   $18$

✎ *Simplify.*

5) $3\sqrt{5} + 2\sqrt{5} =$

6) $6\sqrt{3} + 4\sqrt{27} =$

7) $5\sqrt{2} + 10\sqrt{18} =$

8) $7\sqrt{2} - 5\sqrt{8} =$   $-3\sqrt{2}$

✎ *Evaluate.*

9) $\sqrt{5} \times \sqrt{3} =$

10) $\sqrt{6} \times \sqrt{8} =$

11) $3\sqrt{5} \times \sqrt{9} =$

12) $2\sqrt{3} \times 3\sqrt{7} =$

✎ *Simplify.*

13) $\frac{1}{\sqrt{3}-6} =$

14) $\frac{5}{\sqrt{2}+7} =$

15) $\frac{\sqrt{3}}{1-\sqrt{6}} =$

16) $\frac{2}{\sqrt{3}+5} =$   $\frac{-\sqrt{3}-5}{11}$

✎ *Solve for $x$.*

17) $\sqrt{x} + 2 = 9$

18) $3 + \sqrt{x} = 12$

19) $\sqrt{x} + 5 = 30$   $625$

20) $\sqrt{x} - 9 = 27$

21) $10 = \sqrt{x+1}$

22) $\sqrt{x+4} = 3$

✎ *Identify the domain and range of each function.*

23) $y = \sqrt{x+2} - 1$

24) $y = \sqrt{x+1}$

25) $y = \sqrt{x-4}$

26) $y = \sqrt{x-3} + 1$

$x \geq 3$   $y \geq 1$

# Answers – Chapter 16

1) $16\sqrt{y}$

2) $30$

3) $12a\sqrt{b}$

4) $18$

5) $5\sqrt{5}$

6) $18\sqrt{3}$

7) $35\sqrt{2}$

8) $-3\sqrt{2}$

9) $\sqrt{15}$

10) $\sqrt{48} = 4\sqrt{3}$

11) $9\sqrt{5}$

12) $6\sqrt{21}$

13) $-\dfrac{\sqrt{3}+6}{33}$

14) $-\dfrac{5(\sqrt{2}-7)}{47}$

15) $-\dfrac{\sqrt{3}+3\sqrt{2}}{5}$

16) $-\dfrac{\sqrt{3}-5}{11}$

17) $x = 49$

18) $x = 81$

19) $x = 625$

20) $x = 1,296$

21) $x = 99$

22) $x = 5$

23) $x \geq -2, y \geq -1$

24) $x \geq -1, y \geq 0$

25) $x \geq 4, y \geq 0$

26) $x \geq 3, y \geq 1$

# Chapter 17:

# Logarithms

---

**Math topics that you'll learn in this chapter:**

- ✓ Properties of Logarithms

- ✓ Evaluating Logarithm

- ✓ Natural Logarithm

- ✓ Solving Logarithmic Equation

# Properties of Logarithms: Condense and Expand

☑ Let's review some logarithms properties:

$a^{log_a b} = b$

$log_a 1 = 0$

$log_a a = 1$

$log_a(x . y) = log_a x + log_a y$

$log_a \frac{x}{y} = log_a x - log_a y$

$log_a \frac{1}{x} = - log_a x$

$log_a x^p = p \ log_a x$

$log_{x^k} x = \frac{1}{x} \ log_a x , for \ k \neq 0$

$log_a x = log_{a^c} x^c$

$log_a x = \frac{1}{log_x a}$

## Examples:

1) **Expand this logarithm.** $log_a (3 \times 5) =$

Use *log* rule: $log_a(x . y) = log_a x + log_a y$

Then: $log_a (3 \times 5) = log_a 3 + log_a 5$

2) **Condense this expression to a single logarithm.** $log_a 2 - log_a 7$

Use *log* rule: $log_a x - log_a y = log_a \frac{x}{y}$

Then: $log_a 2 - log_a 7 = log_a \frac{2}{7}$

3) **Expand this logarithm.** $log \left(\frac{1}{7}\right) =$

Use *log* rule: $log_a \frac{1}{x} = - log_a x$

Then: $log \left(\frac{1}{7}\right) = - log 7$

# Evaluating Logarithms

☑ Logarithm is another way of writing exponent. $log_b{}^y = x$ is equivalent to $y = b^x$.

☑ Learn some logarithms rules: ($a > 0, a \neq 0, M > 0, N > 0$, and $k$ is a real number.)

Rule 1: $log_a(M.N) = log_aM + log_aN$     Rule 4: $log_a a = 1$

Rule 2: $log_a\frac{M}{N} = log_aM - log_aN$     Rule 5: $log_a{}^1 = 0$

Rule 3: $log_a(M)^k = klog_aM$     Rule 6: $a^{log_a k} = k$

## Examples:

1) Evaluate: $log_2 32$

   **Solution:** Rewrite 32 in power base form: $32 = 2^5$, then: $log_2 32 = log_2(2^5)$

   Use $log$ rule: $log_a(M)^k = k.log_a(M) \rightarrow log_2(2^5) = 5log_2(2)$

   Use $log$ rule: $log_a(a) = 1 \rightarrow log_2(2) = 1.$   $5log_2(2) = 5 \times 1 = 5$

2) Evaluate: $3log_5 125$

   **Solution:** Rewrite 125 in power base form: $125 = 5^3$, then:

   $log_5 125 = log_5(5^3)$

   Use $log$ rule: $log_a(M)^k = k.log_a(M) \rightarrow log_5(5^3) = 3log_5(5)$

   Use $log$ rule: $log_a(a) = 1 \rightarrow log_5(5) = 1.$   $3 \times 3log_5(5) = 3 \times 3 = 9$

# Natural Logarithms

☑ A natural logarithm is a logarithm that has a special base of the mathematical constant $e$, which is an irrational number approximately equal to $2.71$.

☑ The natural logarithm of $x$ is generally written as $ln\,x$, or $log_e x$.

## Examples:

1) **Solve this equation for** x: $e^x = 6$

**Solution:** If $f(x) = g(x), then: ln(f(x)) = ln(g(x)) \rightarrow ln(e^x) = ln(6)$

Use $log$ rule: $log_a x^b = b\,log_a x \rightarrow ln(e^x) = x\,ln(e) \rightarrow xln(e) = ln(6)$

$ln(e) = 1$, then: $x = ln(6)$

2) **Solve this equation for** x: $ln(4x - 2) = 1$

**Solution:** Use $log$ rule: $a = log_b(b^a) \rightarrow 1 = ln(e^1) = ln(e) \rightarrow ln(4x - 2) = ln\,(e)$

When the logs have the same base: $log_b(f(x)) = log_b(g(x)) \rightarrow f(x) = g(x)$

$ln(4x - 2) = ln(e)$, then: $4x - 2 = e \rightarrow x = \frac{e+2}{4}$

# Solving Logarithmic Equations

☑ Convert the logarithmic equation to an exponential equation when it's possible. (If no base is indicated, the base of the logarithm is 10)

☑ Condense logarithms if you have more than one log on one side of the equation.

☑ Plug in the answers back into the original equation and check to see if the solution works.·

## Examples:

**1) Find the value of $x$ in this equation.** $log_2(36 - x^2) = 4$

**Solution:** Use log rule: $log_b x = log_b y$, then: $x = y$

$4 = log_2(2^4)$, $log_2(36 - x^2) = log_2(2^4) = log_2 16$

Then: $36 - x^2 = 16 \rightarrow 36 - 16 = x^2 \rightarrow x^2 = 20 \rightarrow x = \sqrt{20} = 2\sqrt{5}$

**2) Find the value of $x$ in this equation.** $log(5x + 2) = log(3x - 1)$

**Solution:** When the logs have the same base: $f(x) = g(x), then:$

$ln(f(x)) = ln(g(x))$, $log(5x + 2) = log(3x - 1) \rightarrow 5x + 2 = 3x - 1 \rightarrow 5x + 2 - 3x + 1 = 0 \rightarrow 2x + 3 = 0 \rightarrow 2x = -3 \rightarrow x = -\frac{3}{2}$

Verify Solution: $log(5x + 2) = log(5(-\frac{3}{2}) + 2) = log(-5.5)$

Logarithms of negative numbers are not defined. Therefore, there is no solution for this equation.

# Chapter 17: Practices

 **Expand each logarithm.**

1) $\log_b(2 \times 9) = \log_b 2 + 2\log_b 3$

2) $\log_b(5 \times 7) =$

3) $\log_b(xy) =$

4) $\log_b(2x^2 \times 3y) =$

 **Evaluate each logarithm.**

5) $2\log_9(9) = 2$

6) $3\log_2(8) =$

7) $2\log_5(125) =$

8) $\log_{100}(1) =$

9) $\log_{10}(100) = 2$

10) $3\log_4(16) =$

11) $\frac{1}{2}\log_3(81) =$

12) $\log_7(343) =$

 **Reduce the following expressions to simplest form.**

13) $e^{ln4+ln5} = 20$

14) $e^{ln\left(\frac{9}{e}\right)} =$

15) $e^{ln2+ln7} =$

16) $6\ln(e^5) =$

 **Find the value of the variables in each equation.**

17) $\log_3 8x = 3 \rightarrow x =$ ___

18) $\log_4 2x = 5 \rightarrow x =$ ___

19) $\log_4 5x = 0 \rightarrow x =$ ___

20) $\log 4x = \log 5 \rightarrow x = \frac{5}{4}$

# Answers – Chapter 17

1) $\log_b 2 + 2\log_b 3$

2) $\log_b 5 + \log_b 7$

3) $\log_b x + \log_b y$

4) $\log_b 2 + \log_b x^2 + \log_b 3 + \log_b y$

5) 2

6) 9

7) 6

8) 0

9) 2

10) 6

11) 2

12) 3

13) 20

14) $\frac{9}{e}$

15) 14

16) 30

17) $\frac{27}{8}$

18) 512

19) $\frac{1}{5}$

20) $\frac{5}{4}$

# Chapter 18:

# Circles

**Math topics that you'll learn in this chapter:**

- ✓ Circumference and Area of Circles

- ✓ Arc length and sector Area

- ✓ Equation of a Circle

- ✓ Finding the Center and the Radius of Circles

# Circumference and Area of Circles

☑ In a circle, variable $r$ is usually used for the radius and $d$ for diameter.

☑ *Area of a circle* $= \pi r^2$ ($\pi$ is about 3.14)

☑ *Circumference of a circle* $= 2\pi r$

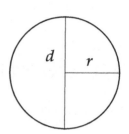

## Examples:

**1) Find the area of this circle.**

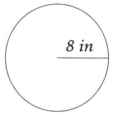

Solution:

Use area formula: $Area = \pi r^2$

$r = 8\ in \rightarrow Area = \pi(8)^2 = 64\pi, \pi = 3.14$

Then: $Area = 64 \times 3.14 = 200.96\ in^2$

**2) Find the Circumference of this circle.**

Solution:

Use Circumference formula: $Circumference = 2\pi r$

$r = 5\ cm \rightarrow Circumference = 2\pi(5) = 10\pi$

$\pi = 3.14$  ***Then:*** $Circumference = 10 \times 3.14 = 31.4\ cm$

**3) Find the area of the circle.**

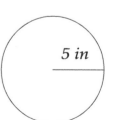

Solution:

Use area formula: $Area = \pi r^2$ ,

$r = 5\ in$ then: $Area = \pi(5)^2 = 25\pi, \pi = 3.14$

***Then:*** $Area = 25 \times 3.14 = 78.5$

**ALEKS Mathematics Prep 2020-2021**

# Arc Length and Sector Area

☑ To find the area of a sector of a circle, use this formula:

Area of a sector $= \pi r^2 (\frac{\theta}{360})$, $r$ is the radius of the circle and $\theta$ is the central angle of the sector.

☑ To find the arc of a sector of a circle, use this formula:

Arc of a sector $= (\frac{\theta}{180})\pi r$

## Examples:

1) **Find the length of the arc. Round your answers to the nearest tenth.** $(\pi = 3.14), r = 20 \, cm, \theta = 30°$

   *Solution:* Use this formula: Length of the sector $= (\frac{\theta}{180})\pi r =$

   $(\frac{30}{180})\pi(20) = (\frac{1}{6})\pi(20) = (\frac{20}{6}) \times 3.14 \cong 10.5 \, cm$

2) **Find the area of the sector.** $(\pi = 3.14)$ $r = 6$ ft, $\theta = 70°$

   **Solution:** Use this formula: area of a sector $= \pi r^2 (\frac{\theta}{360})$

   Area of the sector $= \pi r^2 (\frac{\theta}{360}) = (3.14)(6^2)(\frac{70}{360}) = 21.98 \, \text{ft}^2$

3) **Find the length of the arc.** $(\pi = 3.14)$ $r = 3$ ft, $\theta = \frac{\pi}{3}$

   **Solution:** $\theta = \frac{\pi}{3} \rightarrow \frac{\pi}{3} \times \frac{180}{\pi} = 60°$

   Length of the sector $= (\frac{60}{180})\pi(3) = (\frac{1}{3})\pi(3) = 1 \times 3.14 = 3.14 \, cm$

# Equation of a Circle

☑ Equation of circles in standard form: $(x - h)^2 + (y - k)^2 = r^2$

Center: $(h, k)$, Radius: $r$

☑ Equation of circles in general form: $x^2 + y^2 + Ax + By + C = 0$

## Examples:

**Write the standard form equation of each circle.**

**1)** $x^2 + y^2 - 4x - 6y + 9 = 0$

**Solution:** The standard form of circle equation is: $(x - h)^2 + (y - k)^2 = r^2$ where the radius of the circle is $r$, and it's centered at $(h, k)$.

First, move the loose number to the right side: $x^2 + y^2 - 4x - 6y = -9$

Group $x$-variables and $y$-variables together: $(x^2 - 4x) + (y^2 - 6y) = -9$

Convert $x$ to square form:

$(x^2 - 4x + 4) + y^2 - 6y = -9 + 4 \rightarrow (x - 2)^2 + (y^2 - 6y) = -9 + 4$

Convert $y$ to square form:

$(x - 2)^2 + (y^2 - 6y + 9) = -9 + 4 + 9 \rightarrow (x - 2)^2 + (y - 3)^2 = 4$

Then: $(x - 2)^2 + (y - 3)^2 = 2^2$

**2)** The center of the circle is at $(-2, -10)$, and its radius is 5.

**Solution:** $(x - h)^2 + (y - k)^2 = r^2$ is the circle equation with a radius $r$, centered at $(h, k)$. So, $h = -2$, $k = -10$ and $r = 5$

Then, the equation of the circle is: $(x - (-2))^2 + (y - (-10))^2 = (5)^2$

# Finding the Center and the Radius of Circles

To find the center and the radius of a circle using the equation of the circle:

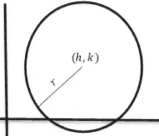

 ☑ Write the equation of the circle in standard form: $(x - h)^2 + (y - k)^2 = r^2$,
 ☑ The center of the circle is at $(h, k)$, and its radius is $r$.

## Examples:

*Identify the center and the radius of each circle.*

**1)** $x^2 + y^2 - 4x + 3 = 0$

**Solution:** $(x - h)^2 + (y - k)^2 = r^2$ is the circle equation with a radius $r$, centered at $(h, k)$.

Rewrite $x^2 + y^2 - 4x + 3 = 0$ in the standard form:

$$x^2 + y^2 - 4x + 3 = 0 \rightarrow (x - 2)^2 + y^2 = 1^2$$

Then, the center is at: $(2, 0)$ and $r = 1$

**2)** $8x + x^2 + 10y = 8 - y^2$

**Solution:** Rewrite the equation in standard form:

$$8x + x^2 + 10y = 8 - y^2 \rightarrow (x - (-4))^2 + (y - (-5))^2 = 7^2$$

Then, the center is at $(-4, -5)$ and the radius is 7.

# Chapter 18: Practices

✍ **Complete the table below.** ($\pi = 3.14$)

1)

|  | Radius | Diameter | Circumference | Area |
|---|---|---|---|---|
| **Circle 1** | 3 inches | 6 inches | 18.84 inches | 28.26 square inches |
| **Circle 2** |  |  | 43.96 meters |  |
| **Circle 3** |  | 8 ft |  |  |
| **Circle 4** |  |  |  | 78.5 square miles |

✍ **Find the length of each arc. Round your answers to the nearest hundredth.**

2) $r = 4$ cm, $\theta = 28°$ → arc = $1.95$

3) $r = 6$ ft, $\theta = 30°$ → arc =

4) $r = 8$ ft, $\theta = 40°$ → arc =

5) $r = 12$ cm, $\theta = 34°$ → arc = $7.12$

✍ **Write the standard form equation of each circle.**

6) $x^2 + y^2 - 4x + 2y - 4 = 0$ → $3^2$

7) $x^2 + y^2 - 8x + 6y - 11 = 0$ →

8) $x^2 + y^2 - 10x - 12y + 12 = 0$ →

9) $x^2 + y^2 + 12x - 6y - 19 = 0$ →

10) $x^2 + y^2 - 6x + 8y + 24 = 0$ →

✍ **Identify the center and radius of each circle.**

11) $(x + 1)^2 + (y - 2)^2 = 5$ → Center: (___,___) Radius: _____

12) $(x - 5)^2 + (y + 10)^2 = 4$ → Center: (___,___) Radius: _____

13) $x^2 + (y - 3)^2 = 8$ → Center: ($0,3$) Radius: $2\sqrt{2}$

14) $(x - 1)^2 + y^2 = 9$ → Center: (___,___) Radius: _____

15) $x^2 + y^2 = 16$ → Center: (___,___) Radius: _____

16) $(x + 1)^2 + (y + 6)^2 = 10$ → Center: (___,___) Radius: _____

# Answers – Chapter 18

1)

|  | Radius | Diameter | Circumference | Area |
|---|---|---|---|---|
| Circle 1 | 3 inches | 6 inches | 18.84 inches | 28.26 square inches |
| Circle 2 | 7 meters | 14 meters | 43.96 meters | 153.86 square meters |
| Circle 3 | 4 ft | 8 ft | 25.12 ft | 50.24 square ft |
| Circle 4 | 5 miles | 10 miles | 31.4 miles | 78.5 square miles |

2) $1.95\ cm$

3) $3.14\ ft$

4) $5.58\ ft$

5) $7.12\ cm$

6) $(x - 2)^2 + (y - (-1))^2 = 3^2$

7) $(x - 4)^2 + (y - (-3))^2 = 6^2$

8) $(x - 5)^2 + (y - 6)^2 = 7^2$

9) $(x - (-6))^2 + (y - 3)^2 = 8^2$

10) $(x - 3)^2 + (y - (-4))^2 = 1^2$

11) Center: $(-1, 2)$, Radius: $\sqrt{5}$

12) Center: $(5, -10)$, Radius: $2$

13) Center: $(0, 3)$, Radius: $2\sqrt{2}$

14) Center: $(1, 0)$, Radius: $3$

15) Center: $(0, 0)$, Radius: $4$

16) Center: $(-1, -6)$, Radius: $\sqrt{10}$

# Chapter 19:

# Rational Expressions

**Math topics that you'll learn in this chapter:**

- ✓ Simplifying Complex Fractions
- ✓ Graphing Rational Expressions
- ✓ Adding and Subtracting Rational Expressions
- ✓ Multiplying Rational Expressions
- ✓ Dividing Rational Expressions
- ✓ Rational Equations

# Simplifying Complex Fractions

☑ Convert mixed numbers to improper fractions.

☑ Simplify all fractions.

☑ Write the fraction in the numerator of the main fraction line then write division sign (÷) and the fraction of the denominator.

☑ Use normal method for dividing fractions.

☑ Simplify as needed.

## Example:

Simplify: $\dfrac{\frac{3}{5}}{\frac{2}{25} - \frac{5}{16}}$

**Solution:** First, simplify the denominator: $\dfrac{2}{25} - \dfrac{5}{16} = -\dfrac{93}{400}$, Then: $\dfrac{\frac{3}{5}}{\frac{2}{25} - \frac{5}{16}} = \dfrac{\frac{3}{5}}{-\frac{93}{400}}$

Now, write the complex fraction using the division sign (÷): $\dfrac{\frac{3}{5}}{\frac{93}{400}} = \dfrac{3}{5} \div \left(-\dfrac{93}{400}\right)$

Use the dividing fractions rule: Keep, Change, Flip (keep the first fraction, change the division sign to multiplication, flip the second fraction)

$$\dfrac{3}{5} \div \left(-\dfrac{93}{400}\right) = \dfrac{3}{5} \times \dfrac{400}{93} = -\dfrac{240}{93} = -\dfrac{80}{31} = 2\dfrac{18}{31}$$

# Graphing Rational Functions

✓ A rational expression is a fraction in which the numerator and/or the denominator are polynomials. Examples: $\dfrac{1}{x}, \dfrac{x^2}{x-1}, \dfrac{x^2-x+2}{x^2+5x+1}, \dfrac{m^2+6m-5}{m-2m}$

✓ To graph a rational function:

- Find the vertical asymptotes of the function if there is any. (Vertical asymptotes are vertical lines which correspond to the zeroes of the denominator. The graph will have a vertical asymptote at $x = a$ if the denominator is zero at $x = a$ and the numerator isn't zero at $x = a$)

- Find the horizontal or slant asymptote. (If the numerator has a bigger degree than the denominator, there will be a slant asymptote. To find the slant asymptote, divide the numerator by the denominator using either long division or synthetic division.)

- If the denominator has a bigger degree than the numerator, the horizontal asymptote is the $x$-axes or the line $y = 0$. If they have the same degree, the horizontal asymptote equals the leading coefficient (the coefficient of the largest exponent) of the numerator divided by the leading coefficient of the denominator.

- Find intercepts and plug in some values of $x$ and solve for $y$, then graph the function.

## Example:

**Graph rational function.** $f(x) = \dfrac{x^2-x+2}{x-1}$

**Solution:** First, notice that the graph is in two pieces. Most rational functions have graphs in multiple pieces. Find $y - intercept$ by substituting zero for $x$ and solving for $y$ $(f(x))$: $x = 0 \rightarrow y = \dfrac{x^2-x+2}{x-1} = \dfrac{0^2-0+2}{0-1} = -2$,
$\qquad y - intercept\colon (0,-2)$

Asymptotes of $\dfrac{x^2-x+2}{x-1}$: Vertical: $x = 1$, Slant asymptote:
$y = 2x + 1$

After finding the asymptotes, you can plug in some values for $x$ and solve for $y$. Here is the sketch for this function.

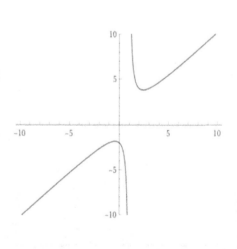

**ALEKS Mathematics Prep 2020-2021**

# Adding and Subtracting Rational Expressions

For adding and subtracting rational expressions:

☑ Find least common denominator (LCD).

☑ Write each expression using the LCD.

☑ Add or subtract the numerators.

☑ Simplify as needed.

## Examples:

**1) Solve.** $\frac{4}{2x+3} + \frac{x-2}{2x+3} =$

**Solution:** The denominators are equal. Then, use fractions addition rule: $\frac{a}{c} \pm \frac{b}{c} = \frac{a \pm b}{c} \rightarrow$

$$\frac{4}{2x+3} + \frac{x-2}{2x+3} = \frac{4+(x-2)}{2x+3} = \frac{x+2}{2x+5}$$

**2) Solve** $\frac{x+4}{x-5} + \frac{x-4}{x+6} =$

**Solution:** Find the least common denominator of $(x-5)$ and $(x+6)$: $(x-5)(x+6)$

Then: $\frac{4}{2x+3} + \frac{x-2}{2x+3} = \frac{(x+4)(x+6)}{(x-5)(x+6)} + \frac{(x-4)(x-5)}{(x+6)(x-5)} = \frac{(x+4)(x+6)+(x-4)(x-5)}{(x+6)(x-5)}$

Expand: $(x+4)(x+6) + (x-4)(x-5) = 2x^2 + x + 44$

Then: $\frac{(x+4)(x+6)+(x-4)(x-5)}{(x+6)(x-5)} = \frac{2x^2+x+44}{(x+6)(x-5)} = \frac{2x^2+x+44}{x^2+x-30}$

# Multiplying Rational Expressions

⊘ Multiplying rational expressions is the same as multiplying fractions. First, multiply numerators and then multiply denominators. Then, simplify as needed.

## Examples:

1) Solve: $\dfrac{x+6}{x-1} \times \dfrac{x-1}{5} =$

**Solution:** Multiply numerators and denominators: $\dfrac{a}{b} \times \dfrac{c}{d} = \dfrac{a \times c}{b \times d}$

$\dfrac{x+6}{x-1} \times \dfrac{x-1}{5} = \dfrac{(x+6)(x-1)}{5(x-1)}$

Cancel the common factor: $(x-1)$

Then: $\dfrac{(x+6)(x-1)}{5(x-1)} = \dfrac{(x+6)}{5}$

2) Solve: $\dfrac{x-2}{x+3} \times \dfrac{2x+6}{x-2} =$

**Solution:** Multiply numerators and denominators: $\dfrac{x-2}{x+3} \times \dfrac{2x+6}{x-2} = \dfrac{(x-2)(2x+6)}{(x+3)(x-2)}$

Cancel the common factor: $\dfrac{(x-2)(2x+6)}{(x+3)(x-2)} = \dfrac{(2x+6)}{(x+3)}$

Factor $2x+6 = 2(x+3)$

Then: $\dfrac{2(x+3)}{(x+3)} = 2$

# Dividing Rational Expressions

✓ To divide rational expression, use the same method we use for dividing fractions. (Keep, Change, Flip)

✓ Keep the first rational expression, change the division sign to multiplication, and flip the numerator and denominator of the second rational expression. Then, multiply numerators and multiply denominators. Simplify as needed.

## Examples:

1) Solve. $\dfrac{x+2}{3x} \div \dfrac{x^2+5x+6}{3x^2+3x} =$

**Solution:** Use fractions division rule: $\dfrac{a}{b} \div \dfrac{c}{d} = \dfrac{a}{b} \times \dfrac{d}{c} = \dfrac{a \times d}{b \times c}$

$\dfrac{x+2}{3x} \div \dfrac{x^2+5x+6}{3x^2+3x} = \dfrac{x+2}{3x} \times \dfrac{3x^2+3x}{x^2+5x+6} = \dfrac{(x+2)(3x^2+3x)}{(3x)(x^2+5x+6)}$

Now, factorize the expressions $3x^2 + 3x$ and $(x^2 + 5x + 6)$. Then:

$3x^2 + 3x = 3x(x+1)$ and $x^2 + 5x + 6 = (x+2)(x+3)$

Simplify: $\dfrac{(x+2)(3x^2+3x)}{(3x)(x^2+5x+6)} = \dfrac{(x+2)(3x)(x+1)}{(3x)(x+2)(x+3)}$, cancel common factors. Then: $\dfrac{(x+2)(3x)(x+1)}{(3x)(x+2)(x+3)} = \dfrac{x+1}{x+3}$

2) Solve. $\dfrac{5x}{x+3} \div \dfrac{x}{2x+6} =$

**Solution:** Use fractions division rule: $\dfrac{a}{b} \div \dfrac{c}{d} = \dfrac{a}{b} \times \dfrac{d}{c} = \dfrac{a \times d}{b \times c}$. Then: $\dfrac{5x}{x+3} \div$

$\dfrac{x}{2x+6} = \dfrac{5x}{x+3} \times \dfrac{2x+6}{x} = \dfrac{5x(2x+6)}{x(x+3)} = \dfrac{5x \times 2(x+3)}{x(x+3)}$

Cancel common factor: $\dfrac{5x \times 2(x+3)}{x(x+3)} = \dfrac{10\ (x+3)}{x(x+3)} = 10$

# Rational Equations

For solving rational equations, we can use following methods:

☑ Converting to a common denominator: In this method, you need to get a common denominator for both sides of the equation. Then, make numerators equal and solve for the variable.

☑ Cross-multiplying: This method is useful when there is only one fraction on each side of the equation. Simply multiply the first numerator by the second denominator and make the result equal to the product of the second numerator and the first denominator.

## Example:

Solve. $\dfrac{x-2}{x+1} = \dfrac{x+4}{x-2}$

Use cross multiply method: if $\dfrac{a}{b} = \dfrac{c}{d}$, then: $a \times d = b \times c$

$$\dfrac{x-2}{x+1} = \dfrac{x+4}{x-2} \rightarrow (x-2)(x-2) = (x+4)(x+1)$$

Expand: $(x-2)^2 = x^2 - 4x + 4$ and $(x+4)(x+1) = x^2 + 5x + 4$, Then:

$x^2 - 4x + 4 = x^2 + 5x + 4$, Now, simplify: $x^2 - 4x = x^2 + 5x$, subtract both

sides $(x^2 + 5x)$, Then: $x^2 - 4x - (x^2 + 5x) = x^2 + 5x - (x^2 + 5x) \rightarrow$

$$-9x = 0 \rightarrow x = 0$$

# Chapter 19: Practices

✎ *Simplify each expression.*

1) $\dfrac{\frac{2}{5}}{\frac{4}{7}} =$

2) $\dfrac{6}{\frac{5}{x}+\frac{2}{3x}} =$ $\dfrac{14x}{17}$

3) $\dfrac{1-\frac{2}{x-1}}{1+\frac{4}{x+1}} =$

4) $\dfrac{x}{\frac{3}{4}-\frac{5}{x}} =$

✎ *Graph rational expressions.*

5) $f(x) = \dfrac{x^2}{5x+6}$

6) $f(x) = \dfrac{x^2+8x+10}{x+5}$

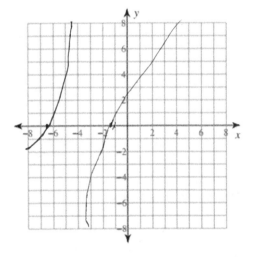

✎ *Simplify each expression.*

7) $\dfrac{5}{x+2} + \dfrac{x-1}{x+2} =$

8) $\dfrac{6}{x+5} - \dfrac{5}{x+5} =$

9) $\dfrac{7}{4x+10} + \dfrac{x-5}{4x+10} =$

✎ *simplify each expression.*

10) $\frac{x+1}{x+5} \times \frac{x+6}{x+1} =$

13) $\frac{x+5}{x+1} \times \frac{x^2}{x+5} =$

11) $\frac{x+4}{x+9} \times \frac{x+9}{x+3} =$   $\frac{x+4}{\cancel{x+3}}$

14) $\frac{x-3}{x+2} \times \frac{2x+4}{x+4} =$

12) $\frac{x+8}{x} \times \frac{2}{x+8} =$

15) $\frac{x-6}{x+3} \times \frac{2x+6}{2x} =$

✎ **Dividing Rational Expressions**

16) $\frac{5x}{4} \div \frac{5}{2} =$

19) $\frac{2}{5x} \div \frac{16}{10} =$

17) $\frac{8}{3x} \div \frac{24}{x} =$   $\frac{1}{4}$

20) $\frac{36}{5} \div \frac{4}{3} =$

18) $\frac{3x}{x+4} \div \frac{x}{3x+12} =$

21) $\frac{15}{6}^{2} \div \frac{5x}{14} =$  7

✎ **Solve each equation.**

22) $\frac{1}{8x^2} = \frac{1}{4x^2} - \frac{1}{x} \rightarrow x =$ ____

23) $\frac{1}{9x^2} + \frac{1}{9x} = \frac{1}{x^2} \rightarrow x =$ ____

24) $\frac{32}{2x^2} + 1 = \frac{8}{x} \rightarrow x =$ ____

25) $\frac{1}{x-5} = \frac{4}{x-5} + 1 \rightarrow x =$ 2

**ALEKS Mathematics Prep 2020-2021**

# Answers – Chapter 19

1) $\frac{7}{10}$

2) $\frac{18x}{17}$

3) $\frac{x^2-2x-3}{x^2+4x-5}$

4) $\frac{4x^2}{3x-20}$

5)

6)

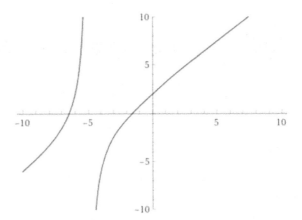

7) $\frac{x+4}{x+2}$

8) $\frac{1}{x+5}$

9) $\frac{x+2}{4x+10}$

10) $\frac{x+6}{x+5}$

11) $\frac{x+4}{x+3}$

12) $\frac{2}{x}$

13) $\frac{x^2}{x+1}$

14) $\frac{2(x-3)}{x+4}$

15) $\frac{x-6}{x}$

16) $\frac{x}{2}$

17) $\frac{1}{9}$

18) $9$

19) $\frac{1}{4}$

20) $\frac{27}{5}$

21) $7$

22) $x = \frac{1}{8}$

23) $x = 8$

24) $x = 4$

25) $x = 2$

# Chapter 20:

# Trigonometric Functions

**Math topics that you'll learn in this Chapter:**

✓ Angle and Angle Measure

✓ Trigonometric Functions

✓ Coterminal Angles and Reference Angles

✓ Evaluating Trigonometric Function

✓ Missing Sides and Angles of a Right Triangle

# Angle and Angle Measure

☑ To convert degrees to radians, use this formula:

$$\text{Radians} = \text{Degrees} \times \frac{\pi}{180}$$

☑ To convert radians to degrees, use this formula:

$$\text{Degrees} = \text{Radians} \times \frac{180}{\pi}$$

## Examples:

**3) Convert 160 degrees to radians.**

**Solution:** Use this formula: $\text{Radians} = \text{Degrees} \times \frac{\pi}{180}$

$$\text{Radians} = 160 \times \frac{\pi}{180} = \frac{160\pi}{180} = \frac{8\pi}{9}$$

**4) Convert $\frac{3\pi}{4}$ to degrees.**

**Solution:** Use this formula: $\text{Degrees} = \text{Radians} \times \frac{180}{\pi}$

$$\text{Radians} = \frac{3\pi}{4} \times \frac{180}{\pi} = \frac{540\pi}{4\pi} = 135$$

# Trigonometric Functions

☑ Trigonometric functions refer to the relation between the sides and angles of a right triangle. There are 6 trigonometric functions:

☑ Sine (sin), Cosine (cos), Tangent (tan), Secant (sec), Cosecant (csc), and Cotangent (cot)

☑ The three main trigonometric functions:

SOH – CAH – TOA, $\sin \theta = \dfrac{opposite}{hypotenuse}$, $Cos\, \theta = \dfrac{adjacent}{hypotenuse}$, $\tan \theta = \dfrac{opposite}{adjacent}$

☑ The reciprocal trigonometric functions:

$$csc\, x = \dfrac{1}{\sin x}, \quad sec\, x = \dfrac{1}{\cos x}, \quad cot\, \theta = \dfrac{1}{\tan x}$$

☑ Learn common trigonometric functions:

| $\theta$ | 0° | 30° | 45° | 60° | 90° |
|---|---|---|---|---|---|
| $\sin \theta$ | 0 | $\dfrac{1}{2}$ | $\dfrac{\sqrt{2}}{2}$ | $\dfrac{\sqrt{3}}{2}$ | 1 |
| $\cos \theta$ | 1 | $\dfrac{\sqrt{3}}{2}$ | $\dfrac{\sqrt{2}}{2}$ | $\dfrac{1}{2}$ | 0 |
| $\tan \theta$ | 0 | $\dfrac{\sqrt{3}}{3}$ | 1 | $\sqrt{3}$ | Undefined |

## Examples:

*Find each trigonometric function.*

1) $\sin 120°$

   **Solution:** Use the following property: $\sin(x) = \cos(90° - x)$

   $\sin 120° = \cos(90° - 120°) = \cos(-30°) = \dfrac{\sqrt{3}}{2}$

2) $\tan 120°$

   **Solution:** Use the following property: $\tan(x) = \dfrac{(x)}{(x)}$

   $$\tan(x) = \dfrac{(x)}{(x)} = \tan(120) = \dfrac{(\quad)}{(\quad)} = \dfrac{\frac{\sqrt{3}}{2}}{-\frac{1}{2}} = -\sqrt{3}$$

**ALEKS Mathematics Prep 2020-2021**

# Coterminal Angles and Reference Angles

☑ Coterminal angles are equal angles.

☑ To find a Coterminal of an angle, add or subtract $360$ degrees (or $2\pi$ for radians) to the given angle.

☑ Reference angle is the smallest angle that you can make from the terminal side of an angle with the x-axis.

## Examples:

1) Find a positive and a negative Coterminal angles to angle $65°$.

**Solution:**

$65° - 360° = -295°$

$65° + 360° = 435°$

$-295°$ and a $435°$ are Coterminal with a $65°$.

2) Find a positive and negative Coterminal angles to angle $\frac{\pi}{2}$.

**Solution:** $\frac{\pi}{2} + 2\pi = \frac{5\pi}{2}$

$\frac{\pi}{2} - 2\pi = -\frac{3\pi}{2}$

3) Find a positive and a negative Coterminal angles to angle $80°$.

**Solution:**

$80° - 360° = -280°$

$80° + 360° = 440°$

$-280°$ and a $440°$ are Coterminal with a $80°$.

# Evaluating Trigonometric Function

✓ Step 1: Find the reference angle. (It is the smallest angle that you can make from the terminal side of an angle with the x-axis.)

✓ Step 2: Determine the quadrant of the function. Depending on the quadrant in which the function lies, the answer will be either be positive or negative.

✓ Step 3: Find the trigonometric function of the reference angle.

## Examples:

1) **Find the exact value of trigonometric function.** $tan \frac{5\pi}{4}$

**Solution:** Rewrite the angle for $\frac{5\pi}{4}$ :

$$tan \frac{5\pi}{4} = tan \left(\frac{4\pi+\pi}{4}\right) = \tan \left(\pi + \frac{1}{4}\pi\right)$$

Use the periodicity of tan: $tan(x + \pi.k) = tan(x)$

$$tan \left(\pi + \frac{1}{4}\pi\right) = tan \left(\frac{1}{4}\pi\right) = 1$$

2) **Find the exact value of trigonometric function.** $cos\ 225°$

**Solution:** *Write* $cos (225°)$ as $cos (135° + 90°)$.

Recall that $cos\ 135° = -\frac{\sqrt{2}}{2}$, $cos\ 90° = 0$

*The reference angle of* $225°$ *is* $90°$. Therefore, $cos\ 90° = 0$

3) **Find the exact value of trigonometric function.** $sin \frac{7\pi}{6}$

**Solution:** Rewrite the angles for $\frac{7\pi}{6}$ :

$$sin \frac{7\pi}{6} = sin \left(\frac{6\pi+\pi}{6}\right) = sin \left(\pi + \frac{1}{6}\pi\right)$$

Use the periodicity of tan: $tan(x + \pi.k) = tan(x)$

$$sin \left(\pi + \frac{1}{6}\pi\right) = sin \left(\frac{1}{6}\pi\right) = \frac{1}{2}$$

# Missing Sides and Angles of a Right Triangle

☑ By using three main trigonometric functions (Sine, Cosine or Tangent), we can find an unknown side in a right triangle when we have one length, and one angle (apart from the right angle).

☑ Adjacent, Opposite and Hypotenuse, in a right triangle is shown below.

☑ Recall the three main trigonometric functions:

SOH – CAH – TOA, $\sin \theta = \frac{opposite}{hypotenuse}$, $Cos\,\theta = \frac{adjacent}{hypotenuse}$, $\tan \theta = \frac{opposite}{adjacent}$

☑ To find missing angles, use inverse of trigonometric functions (examples: $sin^{-1}, cos^{-1}, and\ tan^{-1}$)

# Examples:

1) Find side AC in the following triangle. Round answers to the nearest tenth.

**Solution:** $\sin \theta = \frac{opposite}{hypotenuse}$. $sine\ 50° = \frac{AC}{6} \rightarrow 6 \times \sin 50° = AC$,

Now use a calculator to find $\sin 50°$. $\sin 50° \approx 0.766$

$AC = 6 \times 0.766 = 4.596$, *rounding to the nearest tenth:* $4.596 \approx 4.6$

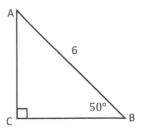

2) Find the value of $x$ in the following triangle.

**Solution:** $\cos \theta = \frac{adjacent}{hypotenuse} \rightarrow \cos x = \frac{10}{14} = \frac{5}{7}$

Use a calculator to find inverse cosine: $cos^{-1}\left(\frac{10}{14}\right) = 44.41° \approx 44°$

Then: $x = 44$

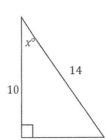

# Chapter 20: Practices

✎ *Convert each degree measure into radians.*

1) $28° =$

2) $80° =$

3) $75° =$

4) $92° =$

✎ **Evaluate.**

5) $sin\ 90° =$ _____

6) $sin\ -330° =$ _____

7) $tan\ -30° =$ _____

8) $cot\frac{2\pi}{3} =$ _____

9) $tan\frac{\pi}{3} =$ _____

10) $sin\frac{2\pi}{6} =$ _____

✎ **Find a positive and a negative Coterminal angles for each angle.**

11) $140° =$

Positive = _____

Negative = _____

12) $-165° =$

Positive = _____

Negative = _____

13) $190° =$

Positive = _____

Negative = _____

14) $\frac{5\pi}{4} =$

Positive = _____

Negative = _____

15) $\frac{2\pi}{9} =$

Positive = _____

Negative = _____

16) $-\frac{7\pi}{9} =$

Positive = _____

Negative = _____

✏️ **Find the exact value of each trigonometric function.**

17) $cos\ 180° =$ _____

18) $cos\ -270° =$ _____

19) $tan\ 225° =$ _____

20) $sin\ \dfrac{\pi}{4} =$ _____

21) $csc\ 330° =$ _____

22) $tan\ -120° =$ _____

✏️ **Find the value** *of* x.

23) _____

26) _____

24) _____

27) _____

25) _____

28) _____

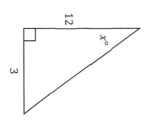

# Answers – Chapter 20

1) $\frac{7}{45}\pi$

2) $\frac{4}{9}\pi$

3) $\frac{5}{12}\pi$

4) $\frac{23}{45}\pi$

5) $1$

6) $\frac{1}{2}$

7) $-\frac{\sqrt{3}}{3}$

8) $-\frac{\sqrt{3}}{3}$

9) $\sqrt{3}$

10) $\frac{\sqrt{3}}{2}$

11) Positive $= 500°$ , Negative $=-220°$

12) Positive $= 195°$ , Negative $=-525°$

13) Positive $= 550°$ , Negative $=-170°$

14) Positive $= \frac{13\pi}{4}$ , Negative $=-\frac{3\pi}{4}$

15) Positive $= \frac{20\pi}{9}$ , Negative $=-\frac{16\pi}{9}$

16) Positive $= \frac{11}{9}$ , Negative $=-\frac{25\pi}{9}$

17) $-1$

18) $0$

19) $1$

20) $\frac{\sqrt{2}}{2}$

21) $-2$

22) $\sqrt{3}$

23)  18

24)  7.8

25)  63

26)  4.5

27)  12.45

28)  14

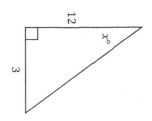

# ALEKS Test Review

ALEKS (Assessment and Learning in Knowledge Spaces) is an artificial intelligence-based assessment tool to measure the strengths and weaknesses of a student's mathematical knowledge. ALEKS is available for a variety of subjects and courses in K-12, Higher Education, and Continuing Education. The findings of ALEKS's assessment test help to find an appropriate level for course placement. The ALEKS math placement assessment ensures students' readiness for particular math courses at colleges.

ALEKS does not use multiple-choice questions like most other standardized tests. Instead, it utilizes adaptable and easy-to-use method that mimic paper and pencil techniques. When taking the ALEKS test, a brief tutorial helps you learn how to use ALEKS answer input tools. You then begin the ALEKS Assessment. In about 30 to 45 minutes, the test measures your current content knowledge by asking 20 to 30 questions. ALEKS is a Computer Adaptive (CA) assessment. It means that each question will be chosen on the basis of answers to all the previous questions. Therefore, each set of assessment questions is unique. The ALEKS Math assessment does not allow you to use a personal calculator. But for some questions ALEKS onscreen calculator button is active and the test taker can use it.

**Key Features of the ALEKS Mathematics Assessment**

Some key features of the ALEKS Math assessment are:

- Mathematics questions on ALEKS are adaptive to identify the student's knowledge from a comprehensive standard curriculum, ranging from basic arithmetic up to precalculus, including trigonometry but not calculus.
- Unlike other standardized tests, the ALEKS assessment does not provide a "grade" or "raw score." Instead, ALEKS identifies which concepts the student has mastered and what topics the student needs to learn.
- ALEKS does not use multiple-choice questions. Instead, students need to produce authentic mathematical input.

**ALEKS Mathematics Prep 2020-2021**

- There is no time limit for taking the ALEKS Math assessment. But it usually takes 30 to 45 minutes to complete the assessment.

The ALEKS Math score is between 1 and 100 and is interpreted as a percentage correct. A higher ALEKS score indicates that the test-taker has mastered more math concepts. ALEKS Math assessment tool evaluates mastery of a comprehensive set of mathematics skills ranging from basic arithmetic up to precalculus, including trigonometry but not calculus. It will place students in classes up to Calculus.

In this book, there are two complete ALEKS Mathematics Tests. Take these tests to simulate the test day experience.

Good luck!

## Time to refine your skill with a practice examination

Take a practice GED Math Test to simulate the test day experience. After you've finished, score your test using the answer key.

## Before You Start

- You'll need a pencil, a calculator, and scratch papers to take the test.

- For these practice tests, don't time yourself. Spend time as much as you need.

- After you've finished the test, review the answer key to check your answers.

**Good luck!**

# ALEKS Mathematics
# Practice Test 1

# 2020 - 2021

**Total number of questions:** 30

**Total time (Calculator):** No time limit

**Calculators are permitted for ALEKS Math Test.**

1) How many tiles of 8 $cm^2$ is needed to cover a floor of dimension 7 $cm$ by 24 $cm$?

21 tiles

2) What is the area of a square whose diagonal is 6 $cm$?

18

3) What is the value of $x$ in the following figure?

155

125°
30°   25   $x°$ 155

4) What is the value of $y$ in the following system of equation?
$$3x - 4y = -20$$
$$-x + 2y = 20$$

$3x - 4y = -20$

$\dfrac{-4y}{-4} = \dfrac{-30 - 3x}{-4}$

$y = \dfrac{-30}{4} - \dfrac{3}{4}x$

190

5) How long does a 420–miles trip take moving at 65 miles per hour $(mph)$?

24

6) When 50% of 60 is added to 12% of 600, the resulting number is:

7) What is the solution of the following inequality?
$$|x - 10| \leq 4$$

8) A bag contains 18 balls: two green, five black, eight blue, a brown, a red and one white. If 17 balls are removed from the bag at random, what is the probability that a brown ball has been removed?

9) If a tree casts a 22–foot shadow at the same time that a 3 feet yardstick casts a 2–foot shadow, what is the height of the tree?

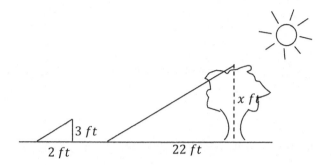

3 ft

2 ft

22 ft

x ft

10) What is the value of $\cos 30°$?

11) Simplify.
$$2x^2 + 4y^5 - x^2 + 2z^3 - 2y^2 + 2x^3 - 2y^5 + 6z^3$$

12) In five successive hours, a car traveled $40\ km, 45\ km, 50\ km, 35\ km$ and $55\ km$. In the next five hours, it traveled with an average speed of $65\ km\ per\ hour$. Find the total distance the car traveled in 10 hours.

13) From last year, the price of gasoline has increased from $1.40 per gallon to $1.75 per gallon. The new price is what percent of the original price?

14) 6 liters of water are poured into an aquarium that's $25cm$ long, $5cm$ wide, and $60cm$ high. How many cm will the water level in the aquarium rise due to this added water? ($1 \; liter \; of \; water = 1,000 \; cm^3$)

15) If a box contains red and blue balls in ratio of $2:3$, how many red balls are there if 75 blue balls are in the box?

16) A chemical solution contains 6% alcohol. If there is $24 \; ml$ of alcohol, what is the volume of the solution?

17) If $\frac{5x}{16} = \frac{x-1}{4}$, $x =$

$-4$

18) Simplify $(-4 + 9i)(3 + 5i)$,

19) If $\tan \theta = \frac{5}{12}$ and $\sin \theta > 0$, then $\cos \theta = ?$

20) If 60% of $x$ equal to 30% of 20, then what is the value of $(x + 7)^2$?

21) A boat sails 80 miles south and then 60 miles east. How far is the boat from its start point?

22) If $x \begin{bmatrix} 2 & 0 \\ 0 & 4 \end{bmatrix} = \begin{bmatrix} x + 3y - 5 & 0 \\ 0 & 2y + 10 \end{bmatrix}$, what is the product of $x$ and $y$?

23) A number is chosen at random from 1 to 20. Find the probability of not selecting a composite number.

24) Removing which of the following numbers will change the average of the numbers to 8?
$$1, 4, 5, 8, 11, 12$$

25) If $y = 4ab + 3b^3$, what is $y$ when $a = 2$ and $b = 4$?

26) If $f(x) = 6 + x$ and $g(x) = -x^2 - 1 - 2x$, then find $(g - f)(x)$.

27) If cotangent of an angel $\beta$ is 2, then the tangent of angle $\beta$ is ...

28) When point $A\ (11, 4)$ is reflected over the $y-$axis to get the point $B$, what are the coordinates of point $B$?

29) If the area of trapezoid is 100, what is the perimeter of the trapezoid?

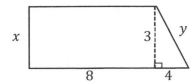

30) If $f(x) = 2x^3 + 5x^2 + 2x$ and $g(x) = -3$, what is the value of $f(g(x))$?

# This is the end of Practice Test 1.

# ALEKS Mathematics
# Practice Test 2

# 2020 - 2021

**Total number of questions:** 30

**Total time (Calculator):** No time limit

**Calculators are permitted for ALEKS Math Test.**

1)  If $f(x) = 4x - 2$ and $g(x) = x^2 - x$, then find $(\frac{f}{g})(x)$.

2)  A bank is offering 4.5% simple interest on a savings account. If you deposit $12,000, how much interest will you earn in two years?

3)  If the ratio of home fans to visiting fans in a crowd is $3:2$ and all 24,000 seats in a stadium are filled, how many visiting fans are in attendance?

4)  If the interior angles of a quadrilateral are in the ratio $2:3:3:4$, what is the measure of the largest angle?

5) If the area of a circle is 49 square meters, what is its diameter?

6) The length of a rectangle is $\frac{5}{4}$ times its width. If the width is 20, what is the perimeter of this rectangle?

7) In the figure below, line $A$ is parallel to line $B$. What is the value of angle $x$?

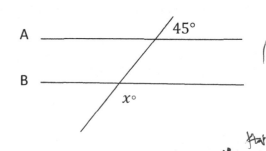

8) An angle is equal to one ninth of its supplement. What is the measure of that angle?

9) What is the value of $y$ in the following system of equations?

$$2x + 5y = 11$$
$$4x - 2y = -14$$

10) Last week 25,000 fans attended a football match. This week three times as many bought tickets, but one sixth of them cancelled their tickets. How many are attending this week?

11) If $sin A = \frac{1}{3}$ in a right triangle and the angle $A$ is an acute angle, then what is $cos A$?

12) In the standard $(x, y)$ coordinate system plane, what is the area of the circle with the following equation?

$$(x + 2)^2 + (y - 4)^2 = 25$$

13) Convert 580,000 to scientific notation.

14) The ratio of boys to girls in a school is 2:3. If there are 500 students in a school, how many boys are in the school.

15) If 150% of a number is 75, then what is 80% of that number?

$$\sin\frac{6\pi}{7}\cos\frac{4\pi}{21} - \cos\frac{6\pi}{7}\sin\frac{4\pi}{21}$$

16) If $A = \begin{bmatrix} -1 & 2 \\ 1 & -2 \end{bmatrix}$ and $B = \begin{bmatrix} 3 & 1 \\ -2 & 3 \end{bmatrix}$, then $2A - B =$

$$y = \frac{5}{2}\cos\left(x + \frac{\pi}{4}\right)$$

17) What is the solution of the following inequality?

$$|x - 2| \geq 4$$

18) If $\tan x = \frac{8}{15}$, then $\sin x =$

19) $(x^6)^{\frac{7}{8}}$ equal to?

20) What are the zeroes of the function $f(x) = x^3 + 5x^2 + 6x$?

$$-\frac{6a - 7x}{5a} + \frac{2a - 3x}{2a} + 2$$

21) If $x + sin^2a + cos^2a = 3$, then $x = ?$

22) If $\sqrt{5x} = \sqrt{y}$, then $x =$

23) The average weight of 18 girls in a class is 55 $kg$ and the average weight of 32 boys in the same class is 62 $kg$. What is the average weight of all the 50 students in that class?

$$e^{Y}=2$$

$$\sqrt[4]{9^{-4x}+8}$$

$$4^2+x^2=9^2$$

$$\log 9^{-x}=8$$

$$16+x^2=91$$

24) What is the value of the expression $5(x - 2y) + (2 - x)^2$ when $x = 3$ and $y = -3$ ?

$$\frac{2\pi}{9}$$

$$\sqrt{x^2}=65$$

$$x=\sqrt{65}$$

$$-\frac{7\pi}{9}$$

$X=0$

$X$

$0.69314718$

$e^{+Y}+$

$23658986 5$

25) Sophia purchased a sofa for $530.40. The sofa is regularly priced at $631. What was the percent discount Sophia received on the sofa?

47

26) If one angle of a right triangle measures 60°, what is the sine of the other acute angle?

$$\left( \cos^{-1}\left( -\frac{4}{5} \right) \right)$$

27) Simplify $\frac{4-3i}{-4i}$ ?

ℓ

$\mathcal{A} + \cos$

$+4$    $\sin = \frac{\sqrt{2}^3}{7}$

28) The average of five consecutive numbers is 40. What is the smallest number?

$(5) \cos \frac{4}{5} (5)$    $+54_5$ $t_9$

$3 \cdot t_4$    $4$    $+5)$

$\sin^{-1}\left( -\frac{\sqrt{3}}{2} \right)$ $5^{+}2_7$    $t_\pi$

$t_\pi$ $t_2$

29) What is the slope of a line that is perpendicular to the line
$$4x - 2y = 14?$$

$-\frac{3}{4}$    $-18_v$

$D = P \times 7$

$6v^4 - 9_v{}^5 - 55_v{}^4$    $11$

$\frac{11}{8}$    $\frac{15}{-18_v}$

30) If $f(x)=2x^3 + 4$ and $(x) = \frac{1}{x}$, what is the value of $f(g(x))$?    $1^{\text{st}}$

$5460 = 6 \times x$

$0.6494075752 \times 12$

$\tan$

$67$

$X$ 

$12$

$\frac{35}{45}$  $\frac{24}{45}$

$\frac{54}{20} \div$

$\frac{15}{9}$  $12$

$1++$

$\frac{105}{135}$  $\frac{7}{9} \div \frac{8}{15}$  $\frac{72}{135}$

$\frac{105}{135} \div \frac{72}{135}$  $\frac{1.458}{1.65}$

$\pi r^2$

# This is the end of Practice Test 2.

$\frac{4}{10}$  $\frac{5}{10}$  $\frac{1}{2} = -\frac{4}{3}w \frac{2}{5}$
$+\frac{2}{5}$    $+\frac{2}{5}$

$\frac{27}{10} \div \frac{-40}{10}$    $27$

$206$  $\frac{a}{10} = \frac{4}{3} w (3)$

$\frac{27}{10} = \frac{4w}{-4}$
$\frac{}{-4}$  $w$

ALEKS Mathematics Prep 2020-2021

# ALEKS Mathematics Practice Tests
# Answers and Explanations

Now, it's time to review your results to see where you went wrong and what areas you need to improve!

## ALEKS Mathematics Practice Test 1

**1) The answer is 21**

The area of the floor is: $7\ cm\ \times 24\ cm = 168\ cm^2$. The number is tiles needed $=$

$$168 \div 8 = 21$$

**2) The answer is 18**

The diagonal of the square is 6. Let $x$ be the side.

Use Pythagorean Theorem: $a^2 + b^2 = c^2$

$x^2 + x^2 = 6^2 \Rightarrow 2x^2 = 6^2 \Rightarrow 2x^2 = 36 \Rightarrow x^2 = 18 \Rightarrow x = \sqrt{18}$

The area of the square is: $\sqrt{18} \times \sqrt{18} = 18$

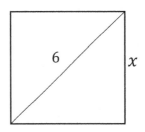

**3) The answer is 155**

$x = 30 + 125 = 155$

**4) The answer is 20**

Solve the system of equations by elimination method.

$3x - 4y = -20$
$-x + 2y = 20$      Multiply the second equation by 3, then add it to the first equation.

$\begin{array}{l} 3x - 4y = -20 \\ 3(-x + 2y = 20) \end{array} \Rightarrow \begin{array}{l} 3x - 4y = -20 \\ -3x + 6y = 60 \end{array} \Rightarrow$ add the equations $2y = 40 \Rightarrow y = 20$

**5) The answer is 6.4 hours**

Use distance formula: $Distance = Rate \times time \Rightarrow 420 = 65 \times T$, divide both sides by

$65. 420 \div 65 = T \Rightarrow T = 6.4\ hours$. Change hours to minutes for the decimal part. $0.4\ hours = 0.4 \times 60 = 24\ minutes$.

**6) The answer is 102**

50% of 60 equals to: $0.50 \times 60 = 30$, 12% of 600 equals to: $0.12 \times 600 = 72$

50% of 60 is added to 12% of 600: $30 + 72 = 102$

7) **The answer is** $6 \leq x \leq 14$

$|x - 10| \leq 4 \rightarrow -4 \leq x - 10 \leq 4 \rightarrow -4 + 10 \leq x - 10 + 10 \leq 4 + 10 \rightarrow 6 \leq x \leq 14$

8) **The answer is** $\frac{17}{18}$

If 17 balls are removed from the bag at random, there will be one ball in the bag. The probability of choosing a brown ball is 1 out of 18. Therefore, the probability of not choosing a brown ball is 17 out of 18 (or $\frac{17}{18}$) and the probability of having not a brown ball after removing 11 balls is the same.

9) **The answer is** $33 \, ft$

**Write a proportion and solve for** $x$. $\frac{3}{2} = \frac{x}{22} \Rightarrow 2x = 3 \times 22 \Rightarrow x = 33 \, ft$

10) **The answer is** $\frac{\sqrt{3}}{2}$

$\cos 30° = \frac{\sqrt{3}}{2}$

11) **The answer is** $2y^5 + 2x^3 + 8z^3 + x^2 - 2y^2$

$2x^2 + 4y^5 - x^2 + 2z^3 - 2y^2 + 2x^3 - 2y^5 + 6z^3$
$= 2x^2 - x^2 + 2x^3 - 2y^2 + 4y^5 - 2y^5 + 2z^3 + 6z^3$
$= x^2 + 2x^3 - 2y^2 + 2y^5 + 8z^3 = 2y^5 + 2x^3 + 8z^3 + x^2 - 2y^2$

12) **The answer is** **550**

Add the first 5 numbers. $40 + 45 + 50 + 35 + 55 = 225$, To find the distance traveled in the next 5 hours, multiply the average by number of hours.

$Distance = Average \times Rate = 65 \times 5 = 325.$   Add both numbers. $325 + 225 = 550$

13) **The answer is** **125%**

The question is this: 1.75 is what percent of 1.40? Use percent formula: $part = \frac{percent}{100} \times whole,$

$1.75 = \frac{percent}{100} \times 1.40 \Rightarrow 1.75 = \frac{percent \times 1.40}{100} \Rightarrow 175 = percent \times 1.40 \Rightarrow percent = \frac{175}{1.40} = 125$

14) **The answer is** **48cm**

$One \, liter = 1,000 \, cm^3 \rightarrow 6 \, liters = 6,000 \, cm^3$   $6,000 = 25 \times 5 \times h \rightarrow h = \frac{6,000}{125} = 48 \, cm$

15) **The answer is** **50**

$\frac{2}{3} \times 75 = 50$

16) **The answer is** $400 \, ml$

6% of the volume of the solution is alcohol. Let $x$ be the volume of the solution.

208

ALEKS Mathematics Prep 2020-2021

Then: $6\%$ of $x = 24\ ml \Rightarrow 0.06\ x = 24 \Rightarrow x = 24 \div 0.06 = 400$

**17) The answer is $-4$**

Solve for $x$. $\frac{5x}{16} = \frac{x-1}{4}$. Multiply the second fraction by 4. $\frac{5x}{16} = \frac{4(x-1)}{4\times4}$. Tow denominators are equal. Therefore, the numerators must be equal. $5x = 4x - 4$,    $5x - 4x = -4$        $-4 = x$

**18) The answer is $-57 + 7i$**

We know that: $i = \sqrt{-1} \Rightarrow i^2 = -1$

$(-4 + 9i)(3 + 5i) = -12 - 20i + 27i + 45i^2 = -12 + 7i - 45 = -57 + 7i$

**19) The answer is $\frac{12}{13}$**

$tan\theta = \frac{\text{opposite}}{\text{adjacent}}$, $tan\theta = \frac{5}{12} \Rightarrow$ we have the following right triangle. Then

$c = \sqrt{5^2 + 12^2} = \sqrt{25 + 144} = \sqrt{169} = 13$

$cos\theta = \dfrac{adjacent}{hypotenuse} = \dfrac{12}{13}$

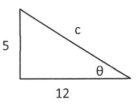

**20) The answer is 289**

$0.6x = (0.3) \times 20 \rightarrow x = 10 \rightarrow (x + 7)^2 = (17)^2 = 289$

**21) The answer is 100 miles**

Use the information provided in the question to draw the shape.

Use Pythagorean Theorem: $a^2 + b^2 = c^2$

$60^2 + 80^2 = c^2 \Rightarrow 3{,}600 + 6{,}400 = c^2 \Rightarrow 10{,}000 = c^2 \Rightarrow c = 100$

80 *miles*

60 *miles*

**22) The answer is 12**

Based on corresponding members from two matrices, we get: $\begin{cases} 2x = x + 3y - 5 \\ 4x = 2y + 10 \end{cases} \rightarrow$

$\begin{cases} x - 3y = -5 \\ 4x - 2y = 10 \end{cases}$, Multiply first equation by $-4$.

$\begin{cases} -4x + 12y = 20 \\ 4x - 2y = 10 \end{cases} \rightarrow$ add two equations. $10y = 30 \rightarrow y = 3 \rightarrow x = 4 \rightarrow x \times y = 12$

**23) The answer is $\frac{9}{20}$**

Set of number that are not composite between 1 and 20: $A = \{1, 2, 3, 5, 7, 11, 13, 17, 19\}$

$Probability = \dfrac{number\ of\ desired\ outcomes}{number\ of\ total\ outcomes} = \dfrac{9}{20}$

**24) The answer is 1**

Let's remove each number and calculate the average.

Remove 1. Then:   $average = \frac{4+5+8+11+12}{5} = \frac{40}{5} = 8$

Remove 4. Then:   $average = \frac{1+5+8+11+12}{5} = \frac{37}{5} = 7.4$

Remove 5. Then:   $average = \frac{1+4+8+11+12}{5} = \frac{36}{5} = 7.2$

Remove 8. Then:   $average = \frac{1+4+5+11+12}{5} = \frac{33}{5} = 6.6$

Remove 11. Then:   $average = \frac{1+4+5+8+12}{5} = \frac{30}{5} = 6$

Remove 12. Then:   $average = \frac{1+4+5+8+11}{5} = \frac{29}{5} = 5.8$

**25) The answer is 224**

$y = 4ab + 3b^3$. Plug in the values of $a$ and $b$ in the equation: $a = 2$ and $b = 4$

$y = 4\,(2)(4) + 3\,(4)^3 = 32 + 3(64) = 32 + 192 = 224$

**26) The answer is $-x^2 - 3x - 7$**

$(g - f)(x) = g(x) - f(x) = (-x^2 - 1 - 2x) - (6 + x)$

$-x^2 - 1 - 2x - 6 - x = -x^2 - 3x - 7$

**27) The answer is $0.5$**

$tangent\ β = \dfrac{1}{cotangent\ β} = \dfrac{1}{2} = 0.5$

**28) The answer is $(-11, 4)$**

When points are reflected over $y$ −axis, the value of $y$ in the coordinates doesn't change and the sign of $x$ changes. Therefore, the coordinates of point $B$ is $(-11, 4)$.

**29) The answer is 35**

The area of trapezoid is: $\left(\frac{8+12}{2}\right) \times x = 100 \rightarrow 10x = 100 \rightarrow x = 10$

$y = \sqrt{3^2 + 4^2} = 5,$   Perimeter is:   $12 + 10 + 8 + 5 = 35$

**30) The answer is $-15$**

$g(x) = -3$, then $f\big(g(x)\big) = f(-3) = 2\,(-3)^3 + 5(-3)^2 + 2(-3) = -54 + 45 - 6 = -15$

# ALEKS Mathematics Practice Test 2

**1)** The answer is $\frac{4x-2}{x^2-x}$

$$\left(\frac{f}{g}\right)(x) = \frac{f(x)}{g(x)} = \frac{4x-2}{x^2-x}$$

**2)** The answer is $1,080$

Use simple interest formula: $I = prt$ ($I =$ interest, $p =$ principal, $r =$ rate, $t =$ time)

$$I = (12,000)(0.045)(2) = 1,080$$

**3)** The answer is $9,600$

Number of visiting fans: $\frac{2 \times 24,000}{5} = 9,600$

**4)** The answer is $120°$

The sum of all angles in a quadrilateral is 360 degrees. Let $x$ be the smallest angle in the quadrilateral. Then the angles are: $2x, 3x, 3x, 4x$, $2x + 3x + 3x + 4x = 360 \rightarrow 12x = 360 \rightarrow x = 30$, The angles in the quadrilateral are: $60°, 90°, 90°$, and $120°$

**5)** The answer is $\frac{7\sqrt{\pi}}{\pi}$

Formula for the area of a circle is: $A = \pi r^2$, Using 49 for the area of the circle we have: $49 = \pi r^2$, Let's solve for the radius $(r)$. $\frac{49}{\pi} = r^2 \rightarrow r = \sqrt{\frac{49}{\pi}} = \frac{7}{\sqrt{\pi}} = \frac{7}{\sqrt{\pi}} \times \frac{\sqrt{\pi}}{\sqrt{\pi}} = \frac{7\sqrt{\pi}}{\pi}$

**6)** The answer is $90$

Length of the rectangle is: $\frac{5}{4} \times 20 = 25$, perimeter of rectangle is: $2 \times (20 + 25) = 90$

**7)** The answer is $135°$

The angle $x$ and 45 are complementary angles. Therefore: $x + 45 = 180 \rightarrow x = 180° - 45° = 135°$

**8)** The answer is $18$

The sum of supplement angles is 180. Let $x$ be that angle. Therefore, $x + 9x = 180$
$10x = 180$, divide both sides by 10: $x = 18$

**9)** The answer is $3$

Solving Systems of Equations by Elimination: Multiply the first equation by $(-2)$, then add it to the second equation.

$$\begin{array}{r} -2(2x + 5y = 11) \\ 4x - 2y = -14 \end{array} \Rightarrow \begin{array}{r} -4x - 10y = -22 \\ 4x - 2y = -14 \end{array} \Rightarrow -12y = -36 \Rightarrow y = 3$$

**10)** The answer is $62,500$

Three times of 25,000 is 75,000. One sixth of them cancelled their tickets. One sixth of 75,000 equals 12,500 ($\frac{1}{6} \times 72,000 = 12,500$). 62,500 ($72,000 - 12,000 = 62,500$) fans are attending this week.

**11) The answer is $\frac{\sqrt{8}}{3}$**

$sinA = \frac{1}{3} \Rightarrow$ Since $sin\theta = \frac{opposite}{hypotenuse}$, we have the following right triangle. Then:

$c = \sqrt{3^2 - 1^2} = \sqrt{9 - 1} = \sqrt{8}, cosA = \frac{\sqrt{8}}{3}$

**12) The answer is $25\pi$**

The equation of a circle in standard form is: $(x - h)^2 + (y - k)^2 = r^2$, where $r$ is the radius of the circle. In this circle the radius is 5. $r^2 = 25 \rightarrow r = 5$, $(x + 2)^2 + (y - 4)^2 = 25$

Area of a circle: $A = \pi r^2 = \pi(5)^2 = 25\pi$

**13) The answer is $5.8 \times 10^5$**

$580,000 = 5.8 \times 10^5$

**14) The answer is 200**

The ratio of boy to girls is $2:3$. Therefore, there are 2 boys out of 5 students. To find the answer, first divide the total number of students by 5, then multiply the result by 2.

$500 \div 5 = 100 \Rightarrow 100 \times 2 = 200$

**15) The answer is 40**

First, find the number. Let $x$ be the number. Write the equation and solve for $x$.

150% of a number is 75, then: $1.5 \times x = 75 \Rightarrow x = 75 \div 1.5 = 50$

80% of 50 is: $0.8 \times 50 = 40$

**16) The answer is $\begin{bmatrix} -5 & 3 \\ 4 & -7 \end{bmatrix}$**

First, find $2A$. $A = \begin{bmatrix} -1 & 2 \\ 1 & -2 \end{bmatrix}$  $2A = 2 \times \begin{bmatrix} -1 & 2 \\ 1 & -2 \end{bmatrix} = \begin{bmatrix} -2 & 4 \\ 2 & -4 \end{bmatrix}$, Now, solve for $2A -$

$B.2A - B = \begin{bmatrix} -2 & 4 \\ 2 & -4 \end{bmatrix} - \begin{bmatrix} 3 & 1 \\ -2 & 3 \end{bmatrix} = \begin{bmatrix} -2 - 3 & 4 - 1 \\ 2 - (-2) & -4 - 3 \end{bmatrix} = \begin{bmatrix} -5 & 3 \\ 4 & -7 \end{bmatrix}$

**17) The answer is $x \geq 6 \cup x \leq -2$**

$x - 2 \geq 4 \rightarrow x \geq 4 + 2 \rightarrow x \geq 6$, Or $x - 2 \leq -4 \rightarrow x \leq -4 + 2 \rightarrow x \leq -2$

Then, solution is: $x \geq 6 \cup x \leq -2$

**18) The answer is $\frac{8}{17}$**

$tan = \frac{opposite}{adjacent}$, and $tan x = \frac{8}{15}$, therefore, the opposite side of the angle $x$ is 8 and the adjacent side is 15. Let's draw the triangle.

Using Pythagorean theorem, we have:

$$a^2 + b^2 = c^2 \rightarrow 8^2 + 15^2 = c^2 \rightarrow 64 + 225 = c^2 \rightarrow c = 17, \sin x = \frac{opposite}{hypotenuse} = \frac{8}{17}$$

**19) The answer is $x^{\frac{21}{4}}$**

$$(x^6)^{\frac{7}{8}} = x^{6 \times \frac{7}{8}} = x^{\frac{42}{8}} = x^{\frac{21}{4}}$$

**20) The answer are $0, -2, -3$**

Frist factor the function: $f(x) = x^3 + 5x^2 + 6x = x(x+2)(x+3)$, To find the zeros, $f(x)$ should be zero. $f(x) = x(x+2)(x+3) = 0$, Therefore, the zeros are: $x = 0, \quad (x+2) = 0 \Rightarrow x = -2,$

$(x+3) = 0 \Rightarrow x = -3$

**21) The answer is 2**

$sin^2 a + cos^2 a = 1$, then: $x + 1 = 3, \qquad x = 2$

**22) The answer is $\frac{y}{5}$**

Solve for $x$. $\sqrt{5x} = \sqrt{y}$. $\qquad$ Square both sides of the equation: $(\sqrt{5x})^2 = (\sqrt{y})^2 \qquad 5x = y$
$$x = \frac{y}{5}$$

**23) The answer is $59.48$**

$average = \frac{sum\ of\ terms}{number\ of\ terms}$, The sum of the weight of all girls is: $18 \times 55 = 990\ kg$

The sum of the weight of all boys is: $32 \times 62 = 1,984\ kg$, The sum of the weight of all students is: $990 + 1,984 = 2,974\ kg$. $average = \frac{2,974}{50} = 59.48$

**24) The answer is 46**

Plug in the value of $x$ and $y$. $x = 3$ and $y = -3$

$$5(x - 2y) + (2 - x)^2 = 5(3 - 2(-3)) + (2 - 3)^2 = 5(3 + 6) + (-1)^2 = 45 + 1 = 46$$

**25) The answer is $16\%$**

The question is this: $530.40$ is what percent of $631$? Use percent formula: $part = \frac{percent}{100} \times whole. 530.40 = \frac{percent}{100} \times 631 \Rightarrow 530.40 = \frac{percent \times 631}{100} \Rightarrow 53,040 = percent \times 631 \Rightarrow percent = \frac{53,040}{631} = 84$. $530.40$ is $84\%$ of $631$. Therefore, the discount is: $100\% - 84\% = 16\%$

**26) The answer is $\frac{1}{2}$**

The relationship among all sides of right triangle $30° - 60° - 90°$ is provided in the following triangle: Sine of $30°$ equals to: $\dfrac{opposite}{hypotenuse} = \dfrac{x}{2x} = \dfrac{1}{2}$

**27) The answer is $\frac{3}{4} + i$**

To simplify the fraction, multiply both numerator and denominator by $i$.

$\dfrac{4-3i}{-4i} \times \dfrac{i}{i} = \dfrac{4i-3i^2}{-4i^2}, i^2 - 1$, Then: $\dfrac{4i-3i^2}{-4i^2} = \dfrac{4i-3(-1)}{-4(-1)} = \dfrac{4i+3}{4} = \dfrac{4i}{4} + \dfrac{3}{4} = \dfrac{3}{4} + i$

**28) The answer is 38**

Let $x$ be the smallest number. Then, these are the numbers: $x, x + 1, x + 2, x + 3, x + 4$

$average = \dfrac{sum\ of\ terms}{number\ of\ terms} \Rightarrow 40 = \dfrac{x+(x+1)+(x+2)+(x+3)+(x+4)}{5} \Rightarrow 40 = \dfrac{5x+10}{5} \Rightarrow$

$200 = 5x + 10 \Rightarrow 190 = 5x \Rightarrow x = 38$

**29) The answer is $-\dfrac{1}{2}$**

The equation of a line in slope intercept form is: $y = mx + b$, Solve for $y$. $4x - 2y = 14 \Rightarrow -2y = 14 - 4x \Rightarrow y = (14 - 4x) \div (-2) \Rightarrow y = 2x - 7$, The slope is 2. The slope of the line perpendicular to this line is: $m_1 \times m_2 = -1 \Rightarrow 2 \times m_2 = -1 \Rightarrow m_2 = -\dfrac{1}{2}$

**30) The answer is $\dfrac{2}{x^3} + 4$**

$f\big(g(x)\big) = 2 \times \left(\dfrac{1}{x}\right)^3 + 4 = \dfrac{2}{x^3} + 4$

## "Effortless Math Education" Publications

Effortless Math authors' team strives to prepare and publish the best quality GED Mathematics learning resources to make learning Math easier for all. We hope that our publications help you learn Math in an effective way and prepare for the GED test.

We all in Effortless Math wish you good luck and successful studies!

Effortless Math Authors

# www.EffortlessMath.com

... So Much More Online!

✓ FREE Math lessons

✓ More Math learning books!

✓ Mathematics Worksheets

✓ Online Math Tutors

**Need a PDF version of this book?**

Visit www.EffortlessMath.com

# Receive the PDF version of this book or get another FREE book!

Thank you for using our Book!

Do you LOVE this book?

Then, you can get the PDF version of this book or another book absolutely FREE!

Please email us at:

info@EffortlessMath.com

for details.

Made in the USA
Coppell, TX
25 May 2021